BRITAIN'S
CONSTITUTIONAL
FUTURE

BRITAIN'S CONSTITUTIONAL FUTURE

Stephen Haseler · Richard Holme
Lord Hunt of Tanworth
David King · Graham Mather
Gerard Radnitzky
Richard Rose · Frank Vibert

Introduction by
Frank Vibert

IEA
Institute of Economic Affairs
1991

First published in November 1991

by

THE INSTITUTE OF ECONOMIC AFFAIRS

2 Lord North Street, Westminster, London SW1P 3LB

© The Institute of Economic Affairs 1991

IEA Readings 36

ISSN 0305-814X
ISBN 0-255 36301-X

The Institute gratefully acknowledges financial support for its publications programme and other work from a generous benefaction by the late Alec and Beryl Warren.

Printed in Great Britain by

Goron Pro-Print Co. Ltd., Lancing, W. Sussex

Filmset in 'Berthold' Times Roman 11 on 12 point

CONTENTS

INTRODUCTION

Frank Vibert
Deputy Director,
Institute of Economic Affairs

THE PUBLICATIONS OF the Institute of Economic Affairs have a long-established tradition of including work on government and the free market. In addition to works on political philosophy, IEA publications have included the thought of Hayek on the framework of government as well as the constitutional economics of public choice theorists. There have also been numerous publications on the rôle of the public sector and its boundary with the free market.

In recent times there have been many who have been ready to declare that the battle for free markets and for limited government has been won. Others are more cautious. They point to the seemingly unstoppable growth in public expenditures and tax burdens relative to economic growth; they point also to the different guises under which markets can be attacked and an expansion in government justified. More fundamentally, they see an unfinished agenda of constitutional and institutional change that must accompany the triumph of market economics if that victory is to be sustained. If the conventions and rules of government are set so as to shield government from being held to account and to disguise government failure; if they fail to hold government institutions in check from their natural inclinations towards a permanent expansion of their rôle; if the voice of government is persistently tuned to extol the virtues of collective choice over individual choice . . ., then recent successes in rolling back the frontiers of the state will prove to be short-lived.

Britain has been at the forefront in the battle for market economics. Constitutional and institutional issues in the United Kingdom have received much less attention. This volume is a step to redress that imbalance and brings together a series of essays on different aspects of constitutional and institutional change in Britain.

The first essay, by Professor Gerard Radnitzky (Professor Emeritus of Philosophy of Science at the University of Trier), presents a brief but illuminating theoretical treatment of the rôle of constitutions from a liberal perspective. Professor Radnitzky defines a constitution in terms of a set of 'master rules' for rule making in collective decisions. They are intended to increase the chances that a society keeps its freedoms. At the same time Professor Radnitzky reminds us that constitutions cannot be an absolute guarantee that societies will remain free. In his view (a view shared by Anthony de Jasay in another recent publication by the Institute of Economic Affairs),[1] the only long-run guarantee of a society's freedom lies in the education of its citizenry and its acceptance of certain norms of political behaviour.

This leads into my own survey of the issues surrounding constitutional reform in the United Kingdom and whether the UK should move towards entrenching its largely unwritten constitutional conventions. Although there is a large measure of consensus in British political life on the virtues of market economics, there is no similar consensus on whether constitutional or institutional reform is needed to accompany the free market. In part this is because, in the British context, the upholders of the free market include followers of the conservative tradition of Burke as well as followers of the British liberal tradition.

The relationship between these two traditions therefore deserves some further brief mention. Both have a common starting point—a belief in the virtues of the evolution of structures rather than artificial constructions according to Burke, and a belief in the virtues of 'spontaneous order' according to the liberal tradition. The unwritten British constitution with its evolutionary history can be seen as representing spontaneous order and thus has virtue from either perspective.

---

[1] A. de Jasay, *Choice, Contract, Consent: A Restatement of Liberalism*, Hobart Paperback No. 30, London: Institute of Economic Affairs, 1991.

The two traditions, however, have rather different criteria when it comes to examining the case for constitutional change. For the Burkeian conservative, social disharmony provides a reason to consider change. The classical liberal, on the other hand, is distrustful of such concepts as social 'harmony', 'cohesion' and 'solidarity', in part because they become an excuse to extend the rôle of government.

Instead, for the liberal there are two key symptoms of systemic failure that provoke the question of the necessity for institutional reform. One symptom is the continual growth of government and shrinking of the area for individual choice and decision. A second symptom is the failure of institutions to provide a stable and predictable framework for rational individual decision-taking. The first phenomenom leads to questions about the possible rôle of constitutional rules or checks and balances as a means to limit the growth of government. The second leads to questions about the signals and incentives to which government institutions respond and the way in which their behaviour may be changed.

The two traditions also differ in their prescriptions for reform. The tradition of Burke offers no abstract ideal towards which institutions should evolve. It is a passive and reactive tradition. On the other hand, the classical liberal tradition does have an interest in rules which limit government, in constitutional constraints on institutions and on those who govern, and in a distrust of unrestrained majoritarianism including that enshrined in the British doctrine of parliamentary sovereignty. The degree to which this interest in rules, checks and balances leads liberals away from 'spontaneous order' towards constitutional constructivism is a source of debate within the liberal tradition. For example, Hayek puts considerable emphasis on rules and the right construction of institutions while Karl Popper put his emphasis on what is learnt through experience rather than on what can be achieved through 'engineering'.

Finally, the two traditions come together again in their view that reform is best achieved by incremental steps and in emphasising that constitutions alone cannot guarantee a free society.[2] Civic behaviour must underpin a culture of freedom. Simply put, this means that individuals must place a continuing value on individual liberties and

---

[2] For an expression of this aspect of the two traditions see, for example, John Gray, *Limited Government: A Positive Agenda*, Hobart Paper No. 113, London: Institute of Economic Affairs, 1989.

on the rules in their society that uphold their freedoms if government is to be held in check.

Professor Stephen Haseler (Professor of Government at City of London Polytechnic), in his essay in this volume, discusses precisely the issue as to whether Britain's constitutional heritage is consistent with a culture of individual freedom. In his view Britain's institutions still represent a paternalistic framework from an earlier age.

The sources of institutional failure in British government underlie the examination by Professor Richard Rose (Centre for the Study of Public Policy, University of Strathclyde) of the British phenomenon of rapid turnover in Ministerial office. Shortness of Ministerial tenure leads to a lack of consistent policy direction and at the same time gives too much leeway to the objectives of the permanent bureaucrats with their interest in the expansion of government. There may be differences of views about the recommendations of Professor Rose for the creation of policy directorates. Some public choice theorists might feel that such a proposal will perpetuate too much power for bureaucrats in the formation of public policy. However, alternatives such as appointing Ministers who are also experts in their subject rather than professional politicians, or conversely the greater use of civil servants in Ministerial capacities, also have important drawbacks considered by Professor Rose.

The changing administrative functions of the civil service touched on by Professor Rose receive a more extensive treatment from Graham Mather. Even with the decentralisation and privatisation of some services hitherto carried out by the state and even with privatisation of state-owned industry, the precise boundary between the public and private sectors remains a source of controversy in Britain and elsewhere. It is not only a question of where the boundary should be drawn but also a question as to how the public sector and private markets interact and relate. The contribution by Graham Mather explores the rôle of contract as a device to mediate between the public and private sectors. The essay points out that such an approach can strengthen the hands of the individual in dealing with government and the public sector. Contract can also provide a mechanism of signals to publicly organised services in cases where market signals are inhibited, and a step towards a fuller rôle for the market.

The essays of both Graham Mather and Professor Rose raise the question of the extent to which the changing nature of the civil service is consistent with traditional doctrines of Parliamentary accountability and Ministerial responsibility. This issue receives treatment in an authoritative essay by Lord Hunt of Tanworth—a former Secretary of the Cabinet. Lord Hunt takes the view that it is possible to reconcile a further decentralisation of government functions with the doctrine of collective Cabinet responsibility. In his view, Treasury control through setting financial limits is not the appropriate means of control. Instead he suggests a broader system of performance monitoring combining service efficiency for the customer with collective Cabinet government.

The structure of the civil service appears malleable in comparison to the seemingly intractable problems of British local government addressed by Dr David King, Senior Lecturer in Economics at Stirling University. Despite attempts to roll back the frontiers of the state, there has at the same time been a progressive increase in the powers of central government at the expense of local government. Dr King stresses the importance of the form, function and finance of local structures being examined as an integrated whole. He poses the question whether local structures can be more than the agents of central government if they do not have their own sources of finance.

Not all observers will agree with the conclusion of Dr King in favour of a local income tax. Public choice theorists might prefer a clearer link between taxes and the exact services organised or supplied by local government, for example through earmarking of taxes or greater use of direct charging. Nevertheless, the essential question posed by Dr King is whether we have achieved the optimum level of government for the carrying out of the functions of government in Britain. It is a question which is also key to the issue of which powers are best exercised in the context of the European Community rather than reserved to Whitehall or Westminster.

In his second contribution to the volume, Professor Richard Rose sets out the issues associated with electoral reform. He draws an important distinction between the representativeness of electoral systems and their practical consequences. He points out that coalition government is the predictable consequence of proportional representation. Some classical liberals will argue that widening the coalition of interests involved in government will reduce the chances of the abuse of power by a narrow section of interests and will make policy less subject to extreme swings. Others will see in coalition government a loss in accountability and an undue influence for otherwise minor interests which might happen to find themselves pivotal in coalition building.

The last word in this volume goes to Lord Holme, Chairman of the Constitutional Reform Centre. His essay on 'Economic and Political Liberalism' brings together many of the themes touched upon by the other authors, including the rôle of local government, justiciable 'rights', the practice of majoritarian rule through the House of Commons, electoral reform and an incremental approach to a written constitutional settlement. He provides a perspective on the practical issues of British constitutional reform. In addition, by reminding us of the broader context of the relationship between political and economic freedoms, Richard Holme brings the reader back in full circle to the theoretical issues of principle first addressed in this volume by Professor Radnitzky.

The relationship between institutional or constitutional structures and economic performance is an inadequately researched area. Yet some of the issues discussed in the volume touch on the question as to whether Britain's relatively modest economic performance in the post-war world is not in part due to our system of government. In part because of dissatisfaction with Britain's relative economic performance and in part because of the importance of issues arising in the context of Britain's membership of the European Community, institutional and constitutional issues in Britain are assuming a new prominence.

The IEA is a research and educational charity. The views expressed in this volume are those of the authors themselves, not of the Institute or its Trustees or Advisers. It is hoped that this collection of essays will provide a useful perspective on some of the issues involved.

October 1991

THE SOCIAL MARKET AND THE CONSTITUTION OF LIBERTY*

Gerard Radnitzky

Emeritus Professor of the Philosophy of Science,
University of Trier

1. Introduction

LIBERAL PHILOSOPHERS believe that one society is less free than another society if in the first society the sector of collective decision relatively to the sector of individual decision is larger than in the second. A crude but handy indicator of the degree of freedom prevalent in a given society is the proportion of taxes in GNP. This measure roughly indicates the extent to which decisions about material resources are made by individuals as individuals.

From the viewpoint of strict liberalism, all contemporary societies could make efforts to come closer to the ideal of the largest possible sector for individual decision. The urgency of the transition from a less free to a more free society varies widely. The societies of East and Central Europe that have recently emerged from a centrally-regulated dictatorship are making great efforts to move towards market-oriented democracies. The Western democracies have for almost a century

*This essay is taken from a longer paper entitled 'The Road to Freedom: The Market before Politics', prepared for the Mont Pèlerin Society. The author wishes to express his sincere thanks to Anthony de Jasay and Arthur Seldon, whose work has been a source of inspiration, and for constructive criticism of an earlier draft. They are of course not responsible for any errors I may have made.

suffered from the growth of government as measured by the growth of state expenditures as a share of the national product. All display an insatiable appetite for publicly provided goods and services and transfer payments. Thus Western democracies also need to roll back the growth of the state to continue the transition to a society of greater individual freedoms.

In political life committed to a free society, the counterpart to a methodology of scientific research is the political philosophy of 'strict liberalism'. That in turn guides the drafting of the Constitution of Liberty. As a counterpart to the methodological rules in research, the Constitution of Liberty offers guidelines that increase the chances of getting closer to the ideal type of a free society. As in the case of the methodology of research, the Constitution *per se* cannot offer any guarantee of success. Ignoring the guidelines provided by the Constitution of Liberty, however, precludes success in the striving for a freer society in the same way as ignoring the methodological rules of rational problem-solving precludes success (scientific progress) in the case of research.

A free society can exist and a transition to a more liberal society can be successful only if liberal ideas get a sufficient number of supporters. For the friends of a free society it is rational to invite everybody to join in their efforts for a transition to a freer society, and to win a critical mass of the population in support of the Constitution of Liberty.

What about the rest? Insofar as it is free-riding and does not oppose the transition, it does no harm. If it does oppose the transition and cannot be convinced that more freedom and prosperity is a good thing, it constitutes a serious practical problem. Appeal to the 'authority' of collective choice or the use of force are certainly not attractive options. Probably the best remedy is competition between states combined with free movement of people and capital. Then people could choose between 'more freedom, higher prosperity, more responsibility and less security' and 'less freedom and prosperity combined with more equality of outcomes and more security'.

2. The Social Market

The label that has been canonised and that best expresses the current mood in Western Europe is 'social market order'. Social Democrats and most, if not all, of the Christian Democrats in Western Europe, particularly in West Germany, have made the concept of 'social market economy' their guiding star. In Germany it has become a sacred cow. No political party would allow its think-tank to conduct a critical analysis of the concept. Such topics are tabooed. The idea of a 'social market economy' is also exportable. On 17 July 1991 the Collegium Budapest was founded. It claimed to be the first Institute for Advanced Study in East Central Europe and it is sponsored by a combination of state agencies and private foundations in an inter-European co-operation. One of its main projects is 'the transition from a centrally-planned economy to a social market economy'. Hence, those who are searching for a transition to a free society need critically to examine the doctrine of 'social market economy'.

The Swedish Model

In the Swedish model of a welfare state, collective decisions have progressively crowded out private decisions and hence freedom of choice. The public sector takes 64 per cent of GNP. Sweden's situation may be epitomised by the formula 'enterprises are free, individuals are socialised'. You are free to start a factory, to sell commodities inside or outside the country, but you are not allowed, for example, to start a school or a radio station, and you would find it very difficult to start a fee-paying alternative to the state health care. The daily life of the citizen has been submerged under a gigantic insurance system, and the welfare system has almost abolished private choice. Sweden illustrates that a maximum of political freedom, understood as democratic institutions throughout, is compatible with very little individual choice. It suggests that if a majority of voters choose social-democratic values the end-result is a loss of individual freedoms. It is not 'socialist' in the sense of a centrally-regulated economy; it is a transfer state legitimised by an egalitarian ideology.

Sweden is generally recognised as an extreme example of the high-tax society. Yet sceptics (or realists?) ask whether other less extreme examples of the 'social market' such as Germany can be rescued from the creeping paralysis caused by the ever-growing intrusion of the state into all walks of life. In the case of Germany, social expenditure in 1990 amounted to almost 30 per cent of GNP—the largest share of public expenditures. The continuous growth of social expenditures progressively reduces the resources left to households for private use. To the direct transfers have to be added the expenditures of enterprises for social benefits as well as the costs (scarcely measurable in monetary terms) of various regulations like protection against dismissal. In September 1991 the German Minister of Economic Affairs drew attention to the costs of various protectionist measures. He pointed out that, for instance, every coal miner's job costs the taxpayer DM76,000 per year in subsidies and special fees on electricity consumption *(Kohlepfennig)*, and that in 1991 the German shipbuilding industry is receiving about DM500 million (about £172 million) from the state. These subsidies are labelled 'competition assistance' *(Wettbewerbshilfen)* and not 'protection against competition', which shows a certain sense of humour.

For the Western democracies to embark on a transition to a larger rôle for the market in a free society would mean recovering some of the ground they have lost. It is well known that at least from the last third of the 19th century—neatly coinciding with the gradual democratisation of politics—one observed in the West a trend towards shifting the public-private balance more and more in favour of collective decisions: the total of government expenditure in GDP grew, and publicly-provided goods tended to crowd out private ones. The state was turned into a vast engine of overt and covert redistribution.

The costly failures of welfare redistribution and their corrosive effects on the fibre of society are increasingly pointed out.[1] Yet there is little sign of any society searching for a transition to more market and less politics, really trying to roll back the tide of creeping socialism. Public choice can easily explain why this is so.[2] 'Majoritarian' democracy tends to maximise the scope of redistributive legislation because of the expected gains from politics. Politicians in such a system are dependent on public opinion. Adherents of a creeping public sector are influential in Western universities, government-owned media, the churches, the welfare administrative apparatus, and the educational system. Socialism, nowadays in creeping or furtive form, remains the justifying ideology of the New Class, the actual and would-be *nomenklatura* of redistribution.

'Social Market Economy', not 'Socialist . . .'

The 'social market' formula has to do with the market order and with redistribution. Let us first distinguish it from 'socialist market

---

[1] A. de Jasay, *Social Contract, Free Ride*, Oxford: The Clarendon Press, 1989, and 'Public Goods: An Appetite That Feeds on Itself', *Economic Affairs*, Vol. 9, No. 6 (August/September 1989).

[2] *Cf.*, for example, G. Tullock, *The Economics of Income Distribution*, Dordrech, Holland: Nijhoff, 1983, and *The Economics of Wealth and Poverty*, Brighton, England: Wheatsheaf Books, 1986.

economy' or 'market socialism'. In full-scale socialism the problem of redistribution does not arise. The state distributes everything, hence *re*distribution would be meaningless. Because the bankruptcy of full-scale socialism can no longer be explained away, avowed socialists operate with the idea of 'market socialism' as a tactical flexible retreat. It is based on the assumption that you can have an efficient economic system without private property rights, and that the problems of information and of motivation can be solved without economic freedom and without a wide distribution of private property rights.

'Market socialism', however, involves a logical inconsistency. 'Market order' (without any qualifying adjective) means efficient allocation based on private property and decentralised decisions. This concept is logically incompatible with the idea of 'socialism'—that is, some (ill-defined) system of non-private ownership and centralised decisions. Once it has been demonstrated that 'market socialism' is a contradiction in terms (a 'square circle', as Anthony de Jasay has called it in a recent study), the concept is no longer of any interest to political philosophy.[3]

Social Market and Redistribution

Leaving aside 'market socialism' and examining instead the 'social market', the core of 'social market' theory concerns redistribution. Redistribution only makes sense if there is an original distribution and that distribution is evaluated as not satisfactory. The various theories legitimising redistribution have two basic arguments:

1. an empirical premise stating that the market order without an adjective (short for free, private market order) is more wealth-creating than any other known system; and

2. a set of value-judgements:
   o prosperity, material wealth, and growth are valued, and hence freedom is implicitly valued for its instrumental value (but not given supremacy in political life), and
   o the state of affairs after redistribution is judged to be preferable to the state of affairs before redistribution.

Thus, while acknowledging the wealth-creating potential of the

---

[3] A. de Jasay, *Market Socialism: A Scrutiny—This Square Circle*, Occasional Paper 84, London: Institute of Economic Affairs, 1990.

free, competitive market, social market theory reverses the doctrine that the market should tame the state. Instead it holds that the state ought to redress the results of market processes—the state should 'tame the market'.

'No-Cost Theory'

There exist three different attempts to justify social market doctrines. The first is a 'no-cost theory'. It states that by practising social market economy, society gains something without losing anything. In its popular form it is a 'you can have your cake and eat it' doctrine. More sophisticated is the version which claims that efficiency can be preserved and the state of affairs 'socially' improved if the redistribution is 'in line with the market' ('*marktkonform*' in the original German coinage of Müller-Armack). Thus, for instance, according to this view, rent control is not in line with the market while subsidies are. This subtype of social market economy doctrine is held by many economists and politicians who make a point of not being socialist.

The assumption underlying this doctrine is false—that is to say, there is no such thing as redistribution in harmony with the market.[4] The additional taxation required to finance the subsidies necessarily increases the difference between the net price (supply price) and the gross price (demand price). The loss in efficiency is furtive, creeping, but in the long run not less than the loss incurred through, for example, rent control.

Theory of Compensated Cost

The second type of justification of the social market is a theory of 'compensated cost'. According to this type of justification, redistribution causes a loss in efficiency, but this cost is necessary for producing 'social peace' or even willing co-operation. Thus, it may in some cases even lead to an increase in efficiency (as, for example, John Rawls claims). It is a version of contractarianism.

The flaw in this version is the practical observation that, if generalised, the underlying assumption is falsified. For instance, massive redistribution in Sweden has led to a noticeable reduction in co-operativeness (for example, absenteeism in Volvo's Gothenburg factory is six times as high as that in Volvo's factory in Belgium).

---

[4] I am indebted to Anthony de Jasay for this point.

Redistribution in Britain in the 1960s and 1970s was accompanied by an increase in the total volume of strikes.

A second flaw and, in my opinion, the main objection to the 'no cost or compensated costs' type of doctrine is that it camouflages the value issue (something that appears to be typical of contractarian theories).

Social market doctrine must admit not only that there are costs in efficiency and freedom resulting from redistribution, but also that it must make the value issue explicit. Only then can the value questions be critically discussed. Any attempt to evade the value issue will involve a variation of the so-called 'naturalistic fallacy'—that is, inferring from the statement that the perverse effects of the welfare state are 'accepted' in the sense of 'socially chosen' (being voted for) the value-judgement that they *should* be acceptable, worthy of being accepted.

'Justified Trade-Off Doctrine'

The third justification of social market doctrine is what might be called the 'justified trade-off doctrine'. It justifies a deliberate trade-off of economic values in the narrow sense of 'economic' (material wealth and efficiency) against realisation of other values (extra-economic values). It should be noted that freedom is not one of these other values because proponents of this version of the social market accept that freedom is necessary for the market to work efficiently.

In the political rhetoric, the pet formula under which these non-economic values are subsumed is 'social justice'. Hayek described this slogan as the best means of destroying our prosperity and freedom.[5] Since nobody can explain what distinguishes 'social justice' from justice, the empty formula is typically construed as more equality of outcome for all groups. Sometimes the accompanying rhetoric may stress 'compassion' or 'caring'; seldom is the reduction of envy mentioned, although envy is a powerful part of its political appeal.

A redistributive fiscal system churns income flows among rent-seeking interest groups 'horizontally' (de Jasay therefore labelled it 'the churning society'), but it does little to help the really poor, who have

---

[5] Hayek has always warned against the 'destructive effects which the invocation of "social justice" has on our moral sensitivity' and told us '... I have come to feel strongly that the greatest service I can still render to my fellow men would be that I could make speakers and writers among them thoroughly ashamed ever again to employ the term "social justice".' (Hayek, *Law, Legislation and Liberty*, Vol. II: *The Mirage of Social Justice*, London: Routledge & Keegan Paul, 1976, p. 97.)

no lobby. Even in its most sophisticated form the doctrine of the social market cannot provide a guiding principle. The doctrine is inconsistent in the sense that the more you realise of prosperity/efficiency the less you can realise (for empirical reasons) of 'social justice' in the sense of equality of outcomes for all groups. The doctrine cannot guide the search for an answer to the problem to which it leads, namely, how to determine the 'right' stopping point, the 'right' trade-off or balance between efficiency and freedom on the one hand and more equality of outcomes on the other. Neither do we know how to justify a value-judgement about the 'right' trade-off or balance.

'A Market of States'

Ideally, if there were a market of states and competition among states for the most productive and innovative human capital, individuals could choose that state in which the placement of the frontier between the domain of private and the domain of collective decision best corresponds to their tastes. If there is no such market of states (or moving costs are evaluated as 'too' high), the problem of how to determine the stopping point has to be solved by collective choice. The advice to stop before the economy is ruined is not helpful. It reminds one of the parable of the villagers who, having built a large city hall with few windows, wanted to have more light (more 'compassion', more equality of outcomes); so they progressively increased the number of windows until eventually the whole structure collapsed. Typically the proposal is made that with the help of the democratic method we can find out the 'right' trade-off. This proposal comes close to the above-mentioned naturalistic fallacy, even if it does not commit it.

The inherent dynamics of the democratic method of collective decision-making refutes this proposal.[6] In an advanced social market democracy the free market will fade away like the Cheshire Cat. Socialism will come in through the back door of majoritarian democracy, and in the long run it will destroy the market order and with it one of the necessary conditions for democracy. In the end the social-democratic compromise will lead to bankruptcy and leave little room for freedom. Ludwig von Mises foresaw this development as early as 1940. He criticised the idea of a social market economy even

---

[6] A. de Jasay, *Social Contract, Free Ride*, Oxford: The Clarendon Press, 1989, and 'A Stocktaking of Perversities', *Critical Review*, Vol. 4, Fall 1990, pp. 437-544.

before it was so christened by the German Christian Democrats. He called the idea 'hampered' market economy.[7] And in the 1966 edition of *Human Action* he concluded:

'Thus the doctrine and practice of interventionism (whose most recent variety is the German *"soziale Marktwirtschaft"*) ultimately tend to abandon what originally distinguished them from outright socialism.'[8]

In summary, the idea of a social market turns out to be a wolf in sheep's (capitalism's) clothing. If it is consistently applied, it will in the long run erode the work ethic, individual responsibility and self-reliance, and society will live off the material fat accumulated in the preceding more capitalist period. The Swedish model is a choice example and the Federal Republic of Germany goes in the same, corporatist direction.

3. The Constitution of Liberty

Among the various possible means that might keep the mandate of government limited but at the same time make sure that it is sufficiently strong to fulfil its protective function, liberals (in the classical sense) look first and foremost to constitutional limitations on the area of collective choice—to minimal rather than to 'limited' government (which is much too vague).

A constitution is basically a system of meta or master rules for rule-making in collective decision. It sets out the 'deontology of the state' outlining 'what the state must, may, and must not do' (Jasay's apt formulation). There is no neutral constitution. Any constitution favours certain identifiable interests.[9] The Constitution of Liberty is intended to increase the chances that society will keep moving towards the ideal type of a free society.

Designing a constitution of liberty is relatively easy compared with the practical problem of making it likely that the constitution will be respected and even defended.[10] If private property rights are protected,

---

[7] In the 1949 English translation of the German original of 1940: L. von Mises, *Human Action: A Treatise of Economics*, London: William Hodge & Co., 1949, p. 714.

[8] L. von Mises, *ibid.*, 3rd revised edition, Chicago: Henry Regnery, 1966, p. 723.

[9] A. de Jasay, 'Is Limited Government Possible?', *Critical Review*, Vol. 3, Spring 1989, pp. 283-309.

[10] For a Hayekian, designing a constitution may perhaps smack too much of social engineering, of constructivism, and it might seem a better alternative to look for ways to make room for spontaneous orders to emerge.

markets will spring up spontaneously. It matters little whether they are legal or illegal; they provide an escape from political coercion. The market will check Leviathan. Nevertheless, when reflecting on a constitution of liberty we have to face tough questions. These include: When is it legitimate from the viewpoint of 'strict liberalism', if it ever is, for some people (princes or parliaments) to coerce others into accepting their choices, e.g., the tax burden they have decided on?[11] Very likely we will have to accept that there will be no optimal constitution, because in practice the choice is between the risks of over-government and under-government. Classical or strict liberals prefer the consequences of too little rather than too much government that even the best princes or politicians would impose.

Principles . . .

The principles guiding the design of a constitution of liberty are not in dispute among liberals. *First*, minimise the rôle of collective choice! This will at the same time reduce the temptation to refer matters to the political process in order to further one's own interest, and thereby reduce the incentives to invest in the political process rather than in productive activities.

Secondly, in the domain of collective choice that appears indispensable, avoid any method of collective choice-making that has a built-in bias that will automatically make the domain of collective choice grow.

Thirdly, redistribution should not be permitted as a means of levelling. Where redistribution is practised in order to assist those in absolute poverty, it should be done in overt form, not in the covert form of publicly provided goods and services, subsidies or other protectionist measures. In summary, the constitution should ensure the sovereignty of the individual not only as earner, saver, and investor, but also, and above all, as consumer. In a free society each citizen as consumer should prevail over himself (herself) as producer (including earner and saver).[12]

Fourthly, changes to the constitution should not be permitted if they reduce 'private rights' such as property rights and freedom of contract.

---

[11] A. de Jasay, *Choice, Contract, Consent: A Restatement of Liberalism*, Hobart Paperback No. 30, London: Institute of Economic Affairs, 1991.

[12] A. Seldon, *Capitalism*, Oxford: Blackwell, 1990, especially p. 121 *et passim*.

... and Outline of an Ideal Constitution

The rough outlines of such an ideal constitution are well known.

(1) The constitution should prohibit budget deficits (whether financed by borrowing or by printing money). Ideally, the monetary constitution should remove government influence from the monetary system and from controlling the stock of money.

(2) Taxation should be treated as a constitutional matter.

(3) There should be constitutional limits to revenues (in times of peace revenues must not exceed a stated percentage of the national income).

(4) Constitutional limits are also required for borrowing, that is, to fund capital projects that constitute productive social investments.

(5) Ideally, the constitution should prohibit direct taxation of income.

(6) Redistribution is permissible only to really 'poor' citizens (poverty being defined in absolute terms—which poses the well-known problem of defining subsistence), not redefined as the relative shortfall from the average income. It should be tackled by constitutional means and not left to majoritarian decision-making (to avoid blackmailing by rent-seeking interest groups).

(7) The constitution should secure the free movement of goods and services, of capital and people.

(8) The constitution should outlaw all sorts of protectionism.

4. The Durability of the Constitution

Creeping socialism is a permanent threat to liberty. This is partly because large segments of the 'intellectual class' favour the growth of government. The more the market replaces politics the less their influence. However, if—*mirabile dictu*—socialism has disappeared, there would still remain a serious threat to freedom, because of the way we conduct democracy now.

Jasay's analysis of the dynamics of democracy provides the following picture. In the framework of a democratic constitution a decisive coalition can get redistributive direct pay-offs through collective decisions (when shaping legislation and imposing policies). Redistributive indirect pay-offs become available from amending the constitution, changing the meta rules with respect to the domain ('what policies may be imposed') and with respect to the size of the decisive coalition ('who is entitled to impose them'). Majorities will soon learn to choose a constitution which maximises the scope for redistributive legislation.[13] Assuming that voters act as rational players maximising pay-offs, the outcome will be an 'unlimited' democracy, popular sovereignty with bare-majority rule and unrestricted domain, the choice rules operating over the entire set of possible alternatives. In unlimited bare-majority democracy:

> 'no minority right subsists without majority consent', and 'no potential winning coalition can hope to augment its redistributive spoils by getting agreement to change the rules (the constitution) any further'.[14]

Whether this end-state is stable or not is unclear. The main point, however, is that democratic dynamics may destroy the best-designed constitution. Concentration of political power (decisive coalitions) will find ways around the political control of the constitution.

Perhaps one can best view a constitution as something like a fortress: a normal garrison with a good fortress has a better chance than what would be the case without the fortress *(ceteris paribus)*, while the fortress makes no difference if the garrison is not willing to defend it. In all cases the constitutional rules must be interpreted to some degree. Whether or not a constitutional court is an advantage will depend upon the integrity of the judges and their commitment to liberty. It may be naïve to assume that they and the people who select them will for long remain unaffected by the climate of opinion.

If people are not disposed to keep its rules, the constitution will be circumvented or changed. A constitution of liberty will have a chance of being respected and 'lived' only so long as the political climate of the country is congenial with its thrust.

In summary, it may be a dangerous illusion to believe that constitutions can protect liberty against a creeping encroachment of the state. Rather than accepting the false sense of security provided by this illusion, it behoves us to seek ways, if there are any, of developing non-illusory defences of liberty.

---

[13] A. de Jasay, 'A Stocktaking of Perversities', *Critical Review*, Vol. 4, Fall 1990, pp. 537-44, especially p. 542.

[14] Jasay, *ibid.*, p. 542.

5. Other Means of Keeping Society on the Road to Freedom

The practical problem is how to achieve a change in the climate of opinion. Educating the public about the political economy of a free society is urgently required in order to create a climate of opinion that will persuade political powers to maintain free markets. Here free-market think-tanks can deliver an educational service that universities do not provide. Pointing out the consequences, the costs of practising the democratic method in the way we have done so far, is part of the task.

Another, perhaps even more important, means is moral education. Respect for truth, for 'promises shall be kept', for property, and so forth, are conventions that provide a valuable social capital. ('*Un curé vaut vingt gendarmes.*') Hence those who wished to undermine property rights, such as the School of Swedish Realism, which forms the intellectual basis of Swedish social democracy, consistently derided the 'taboos of property and contract'. Hayek mentions Gunnar Myrdal as an example.[15] Very likely the only efficient remedy against creeping socialism putting us on the road back to serfdom is a deontological rule that in the political arena gives priority to freedom, to the 'non-domination' principle, and hence accepts the individual's responsibility for his actions. A deontological rule is a rule that prohibits actions of a certain kind independent of the imagined consequences in a particular instance. If a deontological rule guides our behaviour, it is psychologically impossible to do certain things (a 'taboo' on certain kinds of actions such as, for instance, stealing). The rule overrides the pure utility calculus. Do not try to decide on the merits of the case, just exclude certain types of political actions—simply because it is 'psychologically impossible' to break the rule. (For instance, 'A Budget deficit is impossible'—that is, it is not done.) Jasay is probably right when he claims that only such deontological rules can save us.

---

15 Cf. F. A. Hayek, *The Fatal Conceit—The Errors of Socialism* (Vol. I of *The Collected Works*, edited by W. W. Bartley III), London: Routledge, 1988, p. 50.

2

CONSTITUTIONAL REFORM IN THE UNITED KINGDOM
– An Incremental Agenda*

Frank Vibert

Deputy Director,
Institute of Economic Affairs

1. The Revival of Constitutional Reform Proposals

(i) *The reasons for interest*

CONSTITUTIONAL REFORM is a dry subject. Public opinion towards it appears ambiguous. It does not seem to be high on the list of public concerns. On the other hand, in public opinion polls Britain's political institutions, including Westminster, appear to be held in low esteem. Notwithstanding the arid quality of the subject matter, and ambiguous public attitudes, there has taken place a remarkable upsurge of interest in constitutional reform in the United Kingdom within the political parties, public interest groups and the media.

One reason for the rise in interest is purely political. The longevity and commitment to policy reform of the present Conservative administration is resented by those in political disagreement with the agenda. Constitutional reform is seen as a way to fight political battles by other means. From this perspective, it is an agenda for those who are out of power—an agenda for the losers in the political process.

If dissent from conservative policies were the only reason for the

---

*This chapter is a revised version of the paper first published as *IEA Inquiry* No.18 in September 1990.

interest in constitutional reform it would provide a poor rationale for change. There are those who would like to dismiss the pressure for institutional change on this ground alone. The tendency to be dismissive on political grounds may, however, be changing with the swing in political fortunes. It cannot escape notice that the achievements of the Thatcher administrations could be reversed by a different government, not only for political reasons, but also because it is constitutionally possible under the British system of government for the executive in possession of a Parliamentary majority to operate with few institutional restraints.

Leaving policy differences aside, there are three more compelling reasons why constitutional reform is being advocated. The first relates to perceived changes in Britain's institutional practices which individually and collectively are held to give grounds for concern. These include a decline in 'cabinet' government in favour of a more 'presidential' rôle for the Prime Minister; doubts about the effectiveness of Parliamentary scrutiny; a deterioration in relations between central government and local government and between Westminster and the component parts of the United Kingdom; frictions between the government and the media; and more broadly an erosion of the rôle of consensus and convention in British society which in the past provided a stable setting for the exercise of government.

In addition to these and other perceived changes in the practice of British government, a second reason for interest in constitutional reform stems from speculation about the connection between economic performance and forms of government. At its most dramatic this type of connection is illustrated by the revolutions in Central and Eastern Europe. In the British context, continuing frustration with Britain's economic performance relative to other countries in Western Europe—notably Germany—has prompted questions as to whether certain features of Germany's institutions (for example, the greater operational autonomy of the central bank or the greater decentralisation of political life) are associated with superior economic performance. Such comparisons also affect attitudes towards the rôle of the different branches of government. For example, the low quality of educational standards in the United Kingdom in relation to European competitors provides a compelling rationale for central government intervention in educational standards.

The possible connection between institutional structures and economic performance is an elusive one. In extreme cases, as in Eastern and Central Europe, the evidence is that totalitarian régimes cannot remotely satisfy the economic aspirations of the populace. Limited empirical work has also been done on the connection in the case of developing economies.[1] Comparisons between different forms of democratic structures and economic performance (for example, as between Germany and the United Kingdom) are much more difficult to make. The economic success of Japan, for example, is sometimes attributed, at least in part, to the fact that the rôle of the individual is not encouraged but rather the virtues of corporate action. Nevertheless, the connection is an important issue for the conservative tradition because this tradition sees it as essential that government should be market oriented and efficient in both form and function, and because of the importance accorded to the attitudes and aspirations of the individual which are seen to be connected in both the economic and political spheres.

The third reason for the interest in reviewing Britain's constitutional arrangements concerns pressures on British institutions arising from membership of the European Community. The primacy of Community law is a challenge to the traditional British doctrine of Parliamentary sovereignty; policy issues arising in the Community are not regarded as having been effectively handled by Westminster; last but not least, there is growing appreciation that Community treaties are themselves a form of written constitution applicable to Britain over an increasingly wide legislative area. They provide a different type of challenge to Britain's own unwritten conventions.

Moreover, Community treaties do not provide a satisfactory constitutional basis either for Britain or for the new Europe as a whole. Over the coming decade they will need to be reformed in order to provide a more enduring basis for political co-operation in a wider European setting. Britain's case for a decentralised framework for co-operation in Europe that puts individual liberties first has yet to be won against those pressing for moves towards a bureaucratic, unitary state. Demonstration that Britain's own institutions are working well, that procedures for accountability are strong and that political processes in Britain are transparent, is crucial for projection into this broader European debate.

---

[1] Partha Dasgupta, 'Well-being and the Extent of its Realisation in Poor Countries', *Economic Journal*, Supplement 1990, Oxford: Basil Blackwell.

Leaving aside the covert political motivation of some proponents of constitutional reform in the UK, the other classes of reasons for looking afresh at Britain's institutions cannot be ignored. There may be disagreement with particular aspects of the diagnosis. Nevertheless, taken together they provide sufficient explanation why reform proposals are rising to the surface.

(ii) *Conceptual Framework*

In order to evaluate the case for constitutional reform, a conceptual framework is required. The one adopted in this analysis is that of the British conservative tradition. Within this tradition, two distinct approaches lie in uneasy juxtaposition. The first emphasises the values of continuity and those encapsulated in existing institutions and practices. The case for reform, according to this part of the tradition, rests not on a desire for abstract improvements but rather on a pragmatic perception that an existing institution is not working well. It follows that Britain's current constitutional arrangements should be changed only if a pragmatic case can be made about their practical deficiencies. From this perspective the perception that there may be an association between Britain's relatively poor economic performance and its form of government provides a valid reason for looking more closely at current institutional arrangements.

The second approach incorporated within the conservative tradition is the market-oriented legacy of classical liberalism. The overriding theme of this part of the tradition is for the functions of government to be kept to a minimum and for the structures of government to be consistent with its limited rôle. Within this general theme there is an attraction towards a written constitutional framework as a way of providing a set of rules within which the rôle of government institutions is defined and limited, an interest in declarations of individual rights as a way of protecting the individual from the encroachments of government and, related to both aspects, a predilection towards contract and law for defining relationships in society. According to this perspective, the perception that institutional constraints in Britain have weakened *vis à vis* the power of the executive provides a valid reason for examining the case for reform. Thus according to both parts of the British conservative tradition there are good reasons for the case for reform to be examined.

At the same time, as already mentioned, these two parts of the conservative tradition lie uncomfortably together. This is because the continuity of the British experience and the absence of invasions or recent civil strife have resulted in a constitutional evolution without any recently written codification of practices as well as potentially unlimited powers for a government with a Parliamentary majority.

It is sometimes alleged that there is an inherent conflict between these two different aspects of the conservative tradition. There is indeed a philosophical difference between stressing the value of continuity in society, the mystique of symbols, and the power of convention as compared with seeing institutional arrangements as facilitating exchange between political preferences in a manner analogous to commercial exchange in the market-place. However, in practical terms the two aspects of the conservative tradition are not in conflict. Transparency and accountability are key values in both approaches and according to either approach there is a case for constitutional reform in Britain to be addressed. Moreover, both parts of the tradition are relevant. The case for changes in specific institutional arrangements can be assessed on pragmatic grounds according to the one approach. The direction of reforms, in cases where they seem justified, is signposted by the other.

(iii) *Analytic Approach*

There is a notorious gulf between theoretical approaches to constitutional issues and specific institutional questions.[2] The specific suggestions that are being put forward for constitutional change in Britain today, group together ideas (many of long standing) which address very different problems. In order to disentangle the rationale for the reforms being advocated, it is useful to go beyond a general approach and distinguish between the following categories of reform proposals:

o Those proposals which relate to the legitimacy of authority in the British system of government (proposals in this category mainly involve the electoral system).

o Those which address the exercise of authority (for example, those which entail new mechanisms to ensure accountability and transparency in British government).

---

[2] See for example the discussion on 'empty boxes' in John Gray, *Limited Government: A Positive Agenda*, Hobart Paper 113, London: Institute of Economic Affairs, 1989.

○ Role-of-the-state proposals (which attempt to delineate the size and function of the state in the provision of goods and services).

○ Domain-of-governance proposals (which aim to protect the exercise of individual 'rights' and civil liberties within the state).

These different categories are not watertight, but for expositional purposes they help elucidate the different issues involved. Proposals which fall into each of these categories are outlined further below. As already mentioned, it is yet another question as to whether British constitutional practices, reformed or not, should be enshrined in written form. This question is therefore considered separately.

2. Legitimacy of Authority

Historically, much of Britain's constitutional debate centred on the question of the legitimacy of authority in the system of government. The removal of the monarch from government, the removal of all but severely limited powers from the House of Lords, and the requirement for governments to be elected through universal suffrage reflected these debates.

Removing Hereditary Prerogatives

In the main, the constitutional struggles about legitimacy have long since been fought and won. It remains for the vestigial constitutional functions of the Crown to be removed and for the hereditary peerage to lose its rights of membership in the Second Chamber. Most reform proposals would address these final changes. While not without controversy, there can be no serious advocacy of the hereditary principle as relevant to contemporary systems of government. Neither does the removal of the constitutional functions of the Crown mean that the monarchy itself ought to be abolished. For example, an officer elected by one or by both Chambers could give formal assent to legislation and could invite a party leader to form a government or could accept the resignation of a government.

Retaining the monarchy without its constitutional functions would preserve its symbolic rôle as emblem of historical continuity in British life and (as long as it retains popular appeal) as an alternative focus for popular attention away from political leaders. However, the key constitutional function (the selection of government leader) becomes problematic the moment there is not a party with a clear Parliamentary majority. At that moment the Crown is politicised and alternative, transparent, non-monarchical procedures become important. Having the assent function and Prime Ministerial appointment function of the Crown handled in some other way would help protect the monarchy from potentially damaging political entanglement. Insofar as the Crown has a wider constitutional significance it is a negative one—the confusion of the status of the citizen with the status of the subject.

Electoral Reform

The most substantive question concerning the legitimacy of the authority of British government relates to the electoral system. The fact that most post-war governments in Britain have been elected on a minority of votes cast is felt to undermine the legitimacy of their unimpeded ability to carry through major legislative changes with their Parliamentary majority. While this is not a new situation, it has been given new prominence because of the long period in office of the Conservative party combined with its commitment to radical policy reforms. These reforms are felt to lie outside the post-war consensus on the main thrust of policies which was regarded as common to both major parties prior to the Thatcher administration. The fact that policy changes used to take place within a fairly narrow range weakened the case for electoral reform under earlier governments because the possession of political power (or the exclusion from it) was felt to carry much less significance in the presence of a broad consensus on policies.

The same issue of electoral legitimacy has arisen in respect of Westminster's relation to Scotland and Wales. The Government's programme is applied throughout the United Kingdom even though its minority electoral position is even more striking in Scotland and Wales where it has only a small proportion of members of Parliament.

The perceived inequities in Britain's electoral system can be overstated. Representative government does not rest exclusively on electoral majorities. Moreover, there are other factors working to moderate the behaviour of a government in office, including public opinion polls and the desire to be re-elected. Furthermore, it is particularly clear that the desire of some for electoral reform reflects dislike of policies rather than a concern for the constitution. Nevertheless, elections have a unique importance as the means to remove a government from office. Thus imperfect electoral systems strike at the heart of accountability. In addition, legitimacy has a general importance for the association of a government's policies with the support of the populace and in resisting attempted usurpations of power by bodies such as trade unions that represent special interests. Thus electoral reform remains to be addressed. Indeed, it could be thrown into even greater relief if, at the next election, a Conservative government were returned resting more exclusively on its electoral hold in the South of England.

Alternative Electoral Systems

There is no shortage of proposals for alternative electoral systems which would return governments commanding a greater proportion of votes cast. Most involve some form of proportional representation. The traditional objection to such a change is that coalition governments are seen as a likely consequence. This prospect provokes the opposition of those who feel that coalition governments are likely to prove weak and unstable. Moreover, it is felt that the bargaining about positions and policies that accompanies the formation of coalition governments frequently undermines their claim to be representative.

These traditional objections in Britain to coalition governments may be fading as European issues impinge increasingly on political debate because attitudes to Europe's political and economic evolution seem to cut across traditional party lines. Moreover, the experience of other countries with shared party control does not validate any simple conclusion about effective government. The experience in Italy appears negative but not in Germany. Similarly the experience in the United States with party power in Congress different from that in the White House has had both advantages and disadvantages for political processes.

In the final analysis, the obstacle to changing Britain's electoral system is a practical one. No government that has obtained power through one system of elections, or party that sees its opportunity to regain power through that same system, is likely to wish to risk the uncertainties of a new system. This means that proposals for electoral reform are likely to be the perennial fare of minority parties and forever in political limbo.

Pending a political development such as a hung Parliament or a political re-alignment in respect of Europe, which would encourage a re-assessment of the electoral system for the United Kingdom as a whole, there are other less ambitious proposals. Different voting systems could be used in local government elections, for regional assemblies, for the Second Chamber or for the European Parliament. In addition, a government's ability to manipulate the electoral timetable could be reduced by introducing fixed-term elections (although the manipulation of votes of confidence may be used to precipitate elections).

Although criticisms of the British electoral system are exaggerated, perceptions are important—not least for governments committed to a programme of reforms. Of the various approaches to addressing perceptions about the electoral system, perhaps the most promising from a practical point of view would be to introduce an alternative voting system for an elected Second Chamber. Experience with an alternative system in the British context in a limited setting might provide a better basis for judgements about changes which would have a broader impact. This, however, involves taking a view on the rôle of the Second Chamber which is considered next.

3. The Exercise of Authority

(i) *Parliamentary Sovereignty*

The main constitutional question underlying the exercise of government authority in the United Kingdom is the perceived absence of effective checks and balances or other constraints on a government with a Parliamentary majority in the House of Commons. Indeed, some observers see a fundamental conflict between Parliamentary sovereignty as it has evolved in Britain and market-oriented structures of government with their emphasis on constitutional constraints as a means to limit government and protect freedom for the individual. As Hayek once stated:

> 'The triumphant claim of the British Parliament to have become sovereign, and so able to govern subject to no law, may prove to have been the death-knell of both individual freedom and democracy.'[3]

The perceived conflict is not, however, a real one where procedures, practices and convention take the place of other forms of constraint on government. Hayek may have underestimated the importance of Parliamentary procedures and the historical tradition of the House of Commons in opposing arbitrary acts of the executive. Nevertheless,

---

[3] In *New Studies in Philosophy, Politics, Economics and the History of Ideas*, London: Routledge and Kegan Paul, 1978.

the shortcomings of the doctrine of Parliamentary sovereignty are felt to have been put into sharper focus by recent uses of government power and by changes in practice. Moreover, even if the doctrine of Parliamentary sovereignty is accepted, the case can still be made that British practices should be continually examined to ensure that a government can be held to account for its actions and to ensure that the processes of government are fully transparent and open to review.

Leaving aside theoretical perceptions, there are a series of specific observations which are made about the weakness of constraints on a British government backed by a majority in Parliament. Moreover, they come from different sides of the political spectrum. They include:

o the powerlessness of the Parliamentary opposition to block or to carry amendments to legislation;

o the weakness of the House of Commons Committee system as investigative bodies;

o the inadequacy of the Second Chamber;

o government traditions of secrecy which adversely affect the functioning both of Parliament and of the media;

o the lack of operational autonomy of the Bank of England which makes the conduct of economic policy unnecessarily opaque;

o the unsatisfactory state of the division of responsibilities between the central government and local government;

o the frailty of British administrative law.

The picture of over-mighty government, however, is not all one-sided. The civil service still acts as a government within a government. The right balance between Ministers (including the Prime Minister), political and private advisers and the permanent civil service has still not been found. Moreover, the traditional defence of the doctrine of Parliamentary sovereignty still carries some weight. There are entrenched conventions and procedures in the House of Commons which place the government under constant scrutiny and which help protect the rôle of the opposition and the rights of the citizenry at large; and there are traditions and conventions outside the House of Commons (for example, in respect of government relations with the judiciary and the police) which also limit the powers of government.

At the same time, the willingness to rely on tradition and

convention as a check on the powers of government has declined. Some conventions appear to give too much license to government— for example, those that used to be in place between the government and the media no longer seem to reflect the vital rôle played by free media in modern societies. Other conventions have been eroded by outside pressures (for example, normal House of Commons procedures for scrutiny and debate have not dealt effectively with matters pertaining to the European Community). Conventions within British social behaviour which historically have played a crucial rôle between government and governed (for example, the deferential habits of society identified by Bagehot as a key to British political evolution in the last century) have also been eroded. The degree of social consensus has also diminished as Britain has become a more diverse and multi-ethnic society.

The result of the declining rôle and applicability of convention in British political life is that other ways have to be found to hold governments to account for their actions. At the same time, the erosion of consensus as a force in society makes it incumbent to improve the transparency of government. It is the desire to improve the accountability and transparency of government processes that provides the main case for considering certain institutional reforms. It also provides a basis for considering whether Britain would benefit from a written constitution. The question of a written constitution is considered later in this paper. The issue of institutional reforms is considered next.

(ii) *Institutional Proposals*

There are three leading proposals for institutional change which would provide for greater accountability and transparency in British government. The first is for a more effective Second Chamber; the second is for an 'independent' central bank; and the third is for yet another attempt to re-order the relationship between central and local government including regional relationships.

(a) *The Second Chamber*

Britain's Second Chamber, with its mixture of hereditary and appointed members, is a long-standing anomaly. As already mentioned, providing for an elective membership, possibly from central lists of candidates, might provide a useful starting point for electoral reform. Since party lists would probably include candidates who have been appointed life peers, such a system would provide for a degree of continuity in membership between the existing and a reformed Upper House.

The more important aspect, however, and the one which is the main stumbling block to reform, is the question of the powers of the Second Chamber. As presently constituted, the House of Lords carries out mainly an educative and informative function by virtue of the expertise of its appointed members. If its rôle is to extend beyond this and encompass a more substantive legislative function, there would have to be a procedure for the resolving of disputes with the House of Commons. However, those who advocate a bicameral system do not necessarily envisage that the Second Chamber should compete to carry out the same functions as the House of Commons. On the contrary, Hayek amongst others looked to it to perform a different rôle. This appears to be the more fruitful course to explore.

There are several different functions a second chamber might perform which would not lead it into conflict with the House of Commons on the substance or details of specific legislation but which would nevertheless provide for improved government processes. These include:

o a larger rôle in the debate and scrutiny of matters pertaining to Europe and the European Community (particularly if MEPs had rights of attendance);

o a larger rôle in the review of administrative law, delegated legislation and the functioning of bodies operating with delegated powers or with quasi-legal or regulatory (including self-regulatory) authority;

o a rôle in monitoring the application of any new written 'Bill of Rights' if one were introduced, or if the European Convention on Human Rights were to be incorporated into British law;

o a rôle as a constitutional Court if Britain were to adopt a written constitution.

Broadly speaking, these potential functions can be grouped under the heading of monitoring the application of law. It would be a rôle consistent with the traditions of the Upper House and a stronger emphasis on law and contract in British society.

(b) *An 'Independent' Central Bank*

The power of modern governments to manipulate the economy for short-run electoral advantage, or to sway voter interests by expenditures where the tax implications are postponed or concealed, has led market-oriented constitutional theorists to propose that governments should be constrained by monetary or fiscal rules with constitutional force. In practice there is dispute over whether such rules actually work. However, the next best alternative is felt to be provided by central bank 'independence' and this has been suggested for the Bank of England.

Superficially, it is ironic that independence for the Bank of England should be raised as a proposal during a period, not of government profligacy, but while Britain was running a budget surplus. By contrast, the limitations of what can be sought from central bank independence are illustrated by the frustrations of the independent US Federal Reserve confronted by prolonged US budget deficits. Moreover, to couch the issue in terms of central bank 'independence' is misleading since neither the US Fed. nor the German Bundesbank—the two leading examples of so-called 'independent' central banks—are in fact independent of their governments. Both have to heed the political authorities and may be overridden for political reasons (as amply demonstrated recently by the process of German monetary unification). The period of appointment of the Chairman of the US Federal Reserve provides a measure of independence, but political factors still count in the appointment. More important as a constraint both on the central bank and on the government is that public conflict on economic policy between the government and the central bank is damaging to both and to the financial markets. Thus there is a practical premium on finding a *modus vivendi*.

It is also misleading in the opposite direction to suggest that 'independence' would 'only' apply to monetary base control, or 'only' to interest rate policy. Monetary base control, interest rate policy and exchange rate policy are not divisible. The issue therefore is whether it would make sense for this whole area of policy to be the autonomous operational responsibility of the Bank of England, rather than that the responsibility remain internalised within the government.

The case for such a change is, first, that policy could be more efficient because the government would not be involved in the detail of policy implementation. Technical aspects of policy would be depoliticised. Secondly, where the government felt impelled to intervene

27

for some overriding political imperative, or because of a major difference of opinion on economic management, such intervention could be made transparent. It might, for example, require a formal government directive, which in turn might have to be laid before Parliament for inspection and, if necessary, debate. This in itself would be a safeguard against capricious intervention and ensure that intervention was limited to major policy guidelines. In short, proponents of operational autonomy for the Bank of England see advantages in terms both of the quality of monetary management and of procedures for political accountability.

The issue of central bank operational autonomy in the context of Britain alone cannot be compared directly with the questions over independence and political accountability raised in the context of an independent 'Eurofed' in the European Community. Indeed, the Bank of England would have a greater weight in Community institutions if it had a larger rôle in the conduct of British monetary policy and thus could help to underpin decentralised structures in Europe. However, the issues in the context of the Eurofed are of a different order of complexity. On the one hand, the political pressures to pursue relatively lax monetary policies could be acute, not least because the Commission sees itself as performing a political function in the Community and seeks a rôle in the Eurofed. On the other hand, procedures for political accountability are going to be difficult in the extreme to frame. The European Parliament has established no track record in holding the Commission to account for its spending programmes and its efforts in the financial area have been largely devoted to trying to increase Community expenditures rather than to control them. It would be irresponsible of member governments to look to the European Parliament as the primary body charged with holding a Eurofed to account for administering a stable monetary policy. An alternative procedure might be for the central banks of member-states within a Eurofed to report back to their national parliaments and subsequently through member governments to the Council of Ministers. Procedures for greater operational autonomy for the Bank of England would again be entirely consonant with decentralised and evolutionary models of the Eurofed.

(c) *Local and Regional Government*

The relationship between central government and local authorities and between Westminster and Scotland and Wales have been amongst the most vexed areas of government in post-war Britain. Inefficient resource management, misdirected expenditures and a low standard of political accountability have been all too frequent. It has been in order to rectify this situation that the present government has focussed much of its effort towards institutional reform on the problems of local government.

To date the approach has been piecemeal—addressing unrepresentative local bodies or specific functions (such as community care or school management) or funding, on a topic-by-topic basis. The problems, however, are deep-seated and still far from resolved. Although there is a risk that another look at the structure of local and regional government could be disruptive, there *is* a case for yet another attempt to take a unified look at the tiering and functions of local and regional bodies, the spending and taxing patterns to go with them, and the procedures for electoral accountability. This set of inter-related issues should be examined in their entirety rather than being taken piecemeal, in a further effort to re-introduce vigour and responsibility into local, municipal and regional government.

These three areas are not the only ones where Britain's political processes can potentially be made more efficient, more responsive and more transparent. Neither are they new sources of concern. But they are facets of British government where the political and economic pay-off from reform could be high.

4. The Role of the State

The main focus of the present government in reforming Britain's machinery of government has been on trying to limit the functions of government. This achieves several important objectives. It enables the size of the public sector to be reduced; it weakens the power in society of those vested interests, including professional interests, whose rôle has been protected and boosted by the state. It widens the sphere for the expression of individual choice through enlarging the operation of the market. Public claims on resources can be redirected and ideally reduced. A market-oriented approach to the rôle of government emphasises the shifting nature of the public frontier and the necessity to shed old and outdated functions.

There have been some striking successes in rolling back the sphere of government intervention. There is no longer much debate that the state has no rôle as a producer of goods, and it only remains for coal to be denationalised. The state's rôle as provider of directly productive services and infrastructure has also been successfully reduced. Railways remain to be returned to the private sector, leaving an area of dispute in the balance between the state and the private sector in the provision of roads.

Health and Education

Clearly, however, the main area of controversy lies in the rôle of the state in health and education. An increasing rôle for the private sector in delivering these services is thought likely to be associated with a rising cost of services and this in turn aggravates concerns about unequal access, fairness and social divisiveness. In addition, qualitative improvements are difficult to demonstrate in advance of reform. These concerns have to be effectively addressed as the private sector plays a larger rôle. Moreover, as already mentioned, poor standards of education in the United Kingdom, together with low aspirations, inevitably bring the central government into the arena.

Not only have the rôles for the state and the private sector yet to be successfully defined in health and education but, in addition, there are new areas into which the state is being drawn—notably those concerning the environment and the national heritage.

The lesson that might be drawn is not that the struggle to reduce the rôle of the state in Britain is a struggle in vain, but that, on the contrary, if a constant battle is not fought to hold back the boundaries of the state it will indeed become an overwhelming presence.

Law and Order

From a constitutional point of view a traditionally crucial question about the rôle of the state is in relation to the provision of law and order. Perhaps the most pressing is the need for a national police force to operate against certain categories of crime. These include 'serious' crime, financial fraud, computer crime, terrorism and drugs. At the same time, 'oversight' of such a force will have to be resolved. A Committee of the House of Commons or a reconstituted Second House might provide an appropriate mechanism for public accountability.

A second key constitutional issue is the government's relationship to the media. In the United States the media have assumed a rôle equivalent to a fourth branch of the constitution. Whatever criticisms might be made of the media in America, this basic stance is infinitely preferable to regarding the media as in some way (even in a distant way) answerable to the government. In Britain the relationship is still not distant enough. Television has yet to be completely privatised and security concerns in respect of secrecy do not distinguish sharply between disclosure which involves genuine matters of national security and those which simply involve embarrassment to the government of the day.

5. The Domain of Governance

Historically in Britain the House of Commons has been the guardian of individual and civil liberties in society. Moreover, the doctrine of Parliamentary sovereignty implies that disputes in this, as in other controversies, will be resolved through the political process.

Taxation

As one aspect of addressing individual liberties, the Conservative government has used its Parliamentary majority to implement the theme of the government stepping back from unnecessary interference in matters that can be left to individual responsibility and choice. Indeed, it has had a philosophical commitment to the view that government interference erodes the sense of individual responsibility and devalues the moral worth of individuals.

One expression of this theme has been the attempted widening of the range of individual choice by reductions in taxation. While there has been success in reducing direct taxes, the total tax burden has not decreased. Tax reform thus remains on the public policy agenda. In this context there may be a useful rôle for the earmarking of taxes[4] for specific purposes or for the introduction of various forms of charges so that individuals can choose more rationally between public and private services.

Individual and Civil Liberties—A Broader Range

At the same time, for reasons associated with demographic and other social changes, a broader range of issues in individual and civil liberties has been gaining in importance in Britain and elsewhere. Questions over abortion, options to withhold exceptional medical treatment, 'right to die', and protection of personal privacy have all become more prominent in debate. Other aspects of the way in which individuals and society interact, for example involving gender or age discrimination, or sexual preferences, have also gained in prominence. In addition, as

---

[4] Barry Bracewell-Milnes, *The Case for Earmarked Taxes: Government Spending and Public Choice*, Research Monograph 46, London: Institute of Economic Affairs, 1991.

Britain has become an ethnically more diverse society, the question of how to handle a multi-cultural environment (which extends well beyond the question of racial discrimination) cannot be avoided.

Traditionally, government has had a dual rôle in relation to individual and civil freedoms. On the one hand, it is required to refrain from intervention and leave as large a share as possible for the exercise of individual choice and responsibility. On the other hand, it is under pressure to play an active rôle in the securing of individual and civil liberties.

It is exactly because of the inherent tension and contradiction between these two rôles of government that societies have looked to declarations of individual and civil 'rights' as a way to define the rôle of government. Declarations of 'rights' are precisely intended to serve a dual function, both as a way to protect individuals from over-interference by governments, while at the same time providing a guide to activism where action is required in order to secure liberties.

In response to the rising prominence of such topics, as well as to the perception that the Conservative government's approach has been one-sided, there is now a proposal that Britain itself requires a new expression of 'rights'. This can be achieved in three alternative ways: either as part of a broader written constitutional document; or as a self-contained Bill or Charter of Rights; or, thirdly, that the European Convention on Human Rights could be incorporated into British law.

The traditional case against any move in this direction was spelt out at some length by the Attorney General in 1989.[5] *First*, Britain has a unique historical heritage of individual and civil liberties progressively won in which the House of Commons has played the key rôle. The question is why there should be any less reliance on the House of Commons now. If, for example, the programme of the present Government is seen to be deficient in the securing of civil liberties, any such deficiency can be rectified by political means.

Secondly, there is a perceived transformation in the rôle of the judiciary if the Courts are to become the instrument for securing individual and civil rights. Instead of simply applying law, judges will be put in the position of deciding what is best for society over the whole range of topics covered by declarations of rights. The distinction between judges and legislators will be lost.

---

[5] Sir Patrick Mayhew, QC, MP, in a speech to the Society of Conservative Lawyers, October 1989.

Thirdly, the quality of the law will be changed. Once it is seen to have an activist rôle in disputed questions of social and political norms, the impartiality of the law and of judges will be suspect. Judicial appointments will be swayed by political considerations and by the views of appointees on the social and political agenda.

Finally, it could lead to a tussle between the judiciary and Westminster, as well as a legal vacuum, if statutes were struck down by the Courts and Westminster reacted by re-asserting its dominance.

The Role of 'Rights'

The reservations outlined above are clearly fundamental concerns. They also bear on another type of qualification to declarations of rights and that is simply the difficulty of getting prior agreement on the rights themselves. The more extensive the list of rights, the more likely it is that they will be tilted away from their rôle of protecting individuals from government to become a ground for legislative and judicial activism. Declarations of social and economic rights are seen as particularly likely to lead to a massive upsurge in social intervention by the Courts or by the legislature. Probably the most powerful consideration in favour of incorporation of the European Convention on Human Rights into British law is that it is a list of rights that has already been agreed and on which no further debate is necessary. Moreover, the list of rights is a limited list unlikely to be easily exploitable for wholesale intervention in social and economic policy.

At the heart of the matter, however, is the rôle of law and the judiciary in the securing of individual and civil rights. In this context, the reservations expressed about the transformation of the law and the judiciary appear exaggerated in the light of experience in the United States. Despite the political sensitivity of appointments to the Supreme Court of the United States there is no question about the respect in which the Court and its justices are held. Neither can there be any question about the rôle of the Court in consolidating the rule of law or generating respect for the law, despite the areas of controversy into which the Court has been drawn. Particularly in individual and civil liberties it has provided an invaluable adjunct to political processes for resolving disputes in society. It has provided an alternative channel for mediating disputes and as a pressure valve in the system.

The question, therefore, is whether or not it would be useful for the courts in the United Kingdom to accept a similar rôle. An entrenched judicial avenue would give individuals and affected groups an alternative channel for settling their grievances so that there does not have to be exclusive reliance on the House of Commons and political processes. As consensus and convention have lost part of their binding force in British society and as new areas of individual liberties have grown in prominence, the case for a supplementary channel would seem strong.

6. The Case for a Written Constitution

There has recently been a proposal not only that Britain should have a written Bill or Charter of Rights but also a written constitution to replace the unwritten conventions of British constitutional practice. A written constitution would cover the following elements:

○ A description of the main institutions, their functions and prerogatives.

○ An outline of the terms of reference of the various bodies so as to distinguish between their different spheres of responsibility as well as the division of responsibilities between central and local or regional jurisdictions.

○ Stipulations as to the manner of election or appointment of the main institutions, designed to secure their electoral accountability or, in the case of judiciaries, their independence.

○ Declarations of key individual or civil liberties to be secured by the institutions.

There are three main traditional arguments against Britain having a written constitution. First, it is felt that Britain's unwritten conventions have worked quite well in practice and thus there is no case for incorporating them in written form. By contrast, written constitutions may provide merely a façade behind which undemocratic régimes can flourish. Secondly, written constitutions are felt to introduce rigidities into constitutional practice while Britain's own institutions have been able to adapt pragmatically to change. Thirdly, there is the objection already referred to in the case of written expressions of 'rights', that written safeguards are only as good as the judiciary in place to defend them and that there is the likelihood that the law and judiciary will become politicised. Britain is felt to have benefitted by the distinction between the rôle of the courts in applying laws and the rôle of the legislature in making them.

These traditional objections to a written constitution for the United Kingdom have begun to look jaded. First, for the reasons mentioned at the outset of this paper, Britain's institutions are no longer regarded with automatic acclaim. Secondly, written constitutions do not necessarily have to be rigid. Most contain latitude for change through interpretation as well as through procedures for amendment. The key result of a written form is to provide a better guarantee that institutional change is fully debated and does not arrive inadvertently or by gradual accretion. Here, Britain's flexibility may not always be an advantage. Thirdly, in respect of the rôle of the judiciary, it has already been mentioned that a supplementary channel for achieving and validating constitutional objectives may fill a highly valuable function.

'*A More Powerful Form of Codification*'

Not only do the traditional reasons against Britain having a written constitution appear suspect, but also there are good reasons for Britain to consider embodying its conventions in written form. It would provide an occasion for review and overhaul—a review which may in any event be precipitated by strains on the Act of Union. It provides a more powerful form of codification than piecemeal efforts to codify, say, citizens' rights or legislation dealing with the press. It would help buttress institutions and practices not only from erosion within the United Kingdom but from pressures from outside—notably from the European Community. By defining what are the key considerations in Britain's democratic practices, it would help define the deficiencies in Community arrangements and facilitate their reform. It would make political processes in Britain more transparent, particularly in respect of institutional change. It would stand contract and the law in the place of consensus and convention where these have been eroded. At times in its history Britain has found written declarations to be of fundamental value. As Britain and other European states redefine their constitutional relationships, a written constitution for Britain may indeed be timely.

Although these are strong reasons why Britain should depart from convention and consider putting in place a written codification of its constitutional practices and values (including a declaration of rights by reference to the European Convention on Human Rights), it is not something that can be done when there is an unfinished agenda of institutional reform, for example in respect of the Second Chamber. A two-step procedure would therefore seem desirable. The first stage would consist of the implementation of specific institutional reforms, including the incorporation of the European Convention on Human Rights into British law. The second stage would involve the preparation of the constitutional document which would, *inter alia*, reflect the new changes.

7. Conclusions

The present Government has pursued an active agenda of institutional reform in the United Kingdom. It has attempted to limit the rôle of government by taking government out of areas of activities that can be left to the private sector; it has started to address the issue of improved accountability in government by tackling local government reform, and it has put a major emphasis on enlarging the sphere for the exercise of individual choice and responsibility by reducing direct tax burdens and by other measures.

Reviewing the issues of constitutional reform against the perspective of the conservative tradition, it would seem that not only do these efforts require to be continued but, in addition, the reform agenda is a much more extensive one. The primacy of the individual can be emphasised by the incorporation of the European Convention on Human Rights into British law; the theme of accountability can be further pursued in respect of the institutions of central as well as local government, while the transparency of British political processes can be improved by eventual adoption of a written constitution.

Some proponents of constitutional reform in the United Kingdom have a political rather than a constitutional agenda. The case for reform rests on other grounds. Over the coming years political and economic co-operation in Europe will increasingly dominate the agenda of all countries in Europe. Britain must play a leading part in this debate, particularly in respect of the legal and institutional arrangements for co-operation. Themes which are fundamental to democratic habits in the British institutional context must be projected into improved constitutional arrangements in an extended European Community. The values important in British political procedures must be asserted by robust institutions able to withstand centralising and bureaucratic pressures from outside. A more extensive programme of institutional and constitutional reform can help Britain articulate its values and processes more clearly and play a more forceful rôle in this wider European debate.

3

BRITAIN'S FEUDAL CONSTITUTION*

Stephen Haseler

Professor of Government,
City of London Polytechnic;
Co-Chairman, The Radical Society

1. Introduction

ONE OF THE LASTING achievements of the Thatcher era was the establishment of an intellectual proposition: that Britain's decline, and its seemingly endemic uncompetitiveness was, in part at least, the product of the backwardness of our social and political culture. The central idea was that in order to break out of the pattern of decline, Britain had to encourage an 'enterprise culture'; that such an 'enterprise culture' could only be secured by the opening up of British society to the talents and to merit; and that the road to such an open society was blocked on the left by trade union socialism and on the right by aristocratic paternalism.

The 1980s also presented us, starkly, with a choice. We could remain a traditional society, mired in nostalgia, socially immobile and hierarchical, suspicious of change (and of foreigners, even successful ones). Such a traditional society would be cosy, but it would also be poor! Alternatively, we could become a modern capitalist society, competitive and prosperous.

---

*Adapted from a lecture given by Professor Stephen Haseler to the Radical Society in May 1991.

I believe that during the 1980s we hesitantly took that choice. Thatcher's radicalism took on a host of vested interests and began the process of melting the frozen rigidities of British economic and social life. Thatcher's 'enterprise culture' was not universally accepted, but by the end of the 1980s signs of change were all around us. Old attitudes and institutions which had created and sustained deference and dependence were held up to public scrutiny. The universal welfare state, the overblown nationalised industries, the self-destructive trade unions, the complacent and patronising monopoly broadcasters, and even the restrictive practices of the professions: all came out of the 1980s weaker than when they entered.

The Open Society

We took the choice in favour of a modern economy and an open society, and in the process we at least began properly to identify the enemies of the open society—socialism on the one hand, paternalism on the other. Socialism is now effectively stalled. Proving that capitalism was a far greater enemy of class rigidity and social hierarchy than socialism could ever be, undercut the intellectual edge of the left, putting them onto the defensive for over a decade. The worst symptoms of paternalism have also disappeared. The media places the Bertie Wooster, 'Upstairs, Downstairs', forelock-tugging society clearly way in the past.

The rhetoric of politics has changed too. We no longer talk in the old paternalist language, ordering our affairs for an 'officers and men' society. Non-socialist radicalism (and a reborn English liberalism)— forced underground for much of our collectivised and socialised 20th century—is now re-asserting itself. It took Mrs Thatcher to articulate the 'open, classless society' as a national objective. But perhaps her most lasting legacy is to have opened the way for a new generation of political leaders, embodying this new set of more democratic values and manners.

Yet we still have some way to go before we are thoroughly modernised, before an 'open society' becomes a reality rather than an objective. It would be difficult to argue that Britain is, as yet, a mature bourgeois society in the way that the United States or some of the more prosperous Continental countries are. The sad fact is that the paternalistic habit of mind still permeates. Ernest Bevin argued many years ago that the problem with too many of his fellow countrymen was that they exhibited a 'poverty of desire'—desire, that is, to improve and to succeed. We are still too suspicious of success. Citizens are still too bullied by officialdom, consumers too dominated by producers.

Eradicating Paternalism from Britain's Constitution

It is the central proposition of this short paper that the kind of modern liberal democratic society which we opted for in the 1980s ought now to be rounded out by addressing the paternalism—indeed the antiquity—of our constitution. Defenders of the constitutional *status quo* often argue that constitutional reform is unimportant, an irrelevance—that somehow the British are not interested. Yet the way we govern ourselves is crucial, certainly so for the active, responsible kind of citizenship now being advocated by all parties.

Indeed, constitutional change is now back on the agenda. In one of his first speeches John Major placed 'constitutional evolution' at the heart of his message; as one commentator put it:

> 'Constitutional discussion is opening up in the centre and on the libertarian right of British politics as well as the left.'[1]

2. The Arguments for Constitutional Change

The arguments in favour of constitutional change have become overwhelming. *First*, constitutional change flows naturally from the changes of the 1980s. The Tory MP George Walden and others have argued that the very success of Thatcherism in replanting the seeds of economic liberalism and expanding the middle classes means that constitutional change will follow. He has asked:

> 'How can we develop a society of responsible and assertive individuals when our constitutional legacy is based upon superannuated patterns of deference?'[2]

Secondly, constitutional arrangements need to reflect the changing patterns and values of our society. Thus it is not a question of arguing in favour of change for its own sake—only in favour of aligning our constitution with the new realities of life. The fact is that we have an economy and society which is evolving, developing and changing into a modern, democratic capitalist society more like those of our competitors, yet we exist within a constitutional straitjacket, almost a

---

[1] George Walden, CMG, MP, *The Blocked Society*, Tory Reform Group, December 1990, p. 5.

[2] *Ibid.*, p. 5.

time-warp. We are on the verge of the 21st century whilst still possessed of a constitution which resembles a medieval theme-park.

Thirdly, our unreconstructed constitutional framework sends out all the wrong signals. We are seeking to create an open society based upon enterprise and merit, yet we retain a constitution—replete with feudal imagery, arcane and mysterious symbolism, hereditary authority—which promotes utterly different values. We live in a democratic world whilst we inhabit a pre-democratic constitutional framework. An open society needs an open constitution. We tell the East Europeans that they cannot become prosperous without abandoning their post-war political system. This should apply to us, too. There is increasing recognition that constitutions can affect economic performance. The most obvious example is that the different standing of the central banks in Germany and the United States helps to insulate the day-to-day conduct of monetary policy from short-term political considerations.

Fourthly, there is the changing reality of our international position. We are no longer the hub of a world-wide empire, yet we have continued for far too long with an illusion about our standing, encouraged by such fictions as the Commonwealth. The wag's depiction of the Commonwealth as 'nothing in common, and no wealth' about sums it up! A failure to perceive the changes in the relative position of Britain in the world has contributed to an uncritical acceptance of our institutional structures.

Fifthly and finally, there is the looming European dimension. We are in the middle of a European debate about the way we govern ourselves and about constitutions. Who controls our money? What are the powers of the centre and the periphery? Some sceptics argue that attempting to reform Britain is hopeless, that we can achieve a modern polity only through merging ourselves into a new European federal system. They have a point. Yet to have a modern constitution imposed on us would be a defeat. We should do it ourselves.

3. The Constitutional Changes Required

What, then, are the specific suggestions for the next stage of 'constitutional evolution' which flow from all this? We have already seen some interesting ideas emanating from the Thatcherite, neo-liberal political stable. A few months ago Frank Vibert of the Institute of Economic Affairs produced a list. It suggested that the central principles of a modern constitution should be a written constitutional document, an entrenched Bill of Rights, the removal of the hereditary principle in the House of Lords, and the withdrawal of the constitutional importance of the monarchy.[3]

I find myself in agreement with these propositions. And I would like to place my own, more social democratic propositions within the framework of four general principles.

First, a written constitution is required which makes clear that government rests on the people and does not derive legitimacy from above.

Second is the need for citizenship. Citizenship is now a 'buzz word' but none the worse for that. But how can we constantly ask for the development of citizenship when the idea of citizenship is so weakly developed, and technically and constitutionally we are all still subjects rather than citizens? Citizens have rights, and individual rights require to be entrenched. Most modern nations accept this principle, yet this is not the nub of the argument. The key point is that by entrenching individual rights we set firm, inalienable limits on the power and reach of the state and the government.

Thirdly, an open society must have open government. Whitehall is still far too secretive. And the cult of secrecy does not serve—as it should—the necessary protections of national security; rather, all too often it is the cover for the mistakes and scandals of bureaucratic officialdom. This is where Parliament should come in. The Commons does not need to be 'sovereign'. (The last person who wanted to establish 'sovereignty' was Tony Benn in his 1970s enthusiasm for a seige economy in which Britain turned its back on the international trading system. We have moved on since then.) What the Commons does have to be is investigative—to act more like the United States Congress. Why shouldn't the Commons, like the US Senate, review senior judicial appointments? And why shouldn't top civil servants, instead of cowering under ministerial coat-tails, be subject to the rigorous probing of the elected representatives of the people?

Fourthly, a constitutional framework is called for which is truly, indeed systematically, democratic. Thus any new constitutional settlement cannot possibly take place without addressing the hereditary element in the constitution. Thus the House of Lords remains a

---

[3] Frank Vibert, 'Constitutional Reform in the United Kingdom—An Incremental Agenda', Institute of Economic Affairs, *IEA Inquiry* No. 18, September 1990. An edited version of this paper is published as Chapter 2 of this volume.

stubborn obstacle, a monument to pre-democratic, indeed feudal, habits. It will not do to sweep this issue under the carpet, as defenders attempt to, by arguing that our Upper House is an irrelevance. It is not. Many still see it—even at the dawning of the 21st century—as the focal point of ambition. And it still has a rôle, no matter how minimal, in determining the laws which govern a free people.

The fact is that a legislative body (and the House of Lords *is* a legislative body!) in which heredity remains a qualification for membership, in which birth alone is a criterion for helping to determine the laws which govern a free people, is not only an anachronism, but an embarrassment.

And the non-hereditary element in our Upper House also presents modern democrats (let alone radicals) with problems. Much individual talent has been appointed to the Upper House. Yet this is hardly the issue. The reality is that a system which allows unelected persons (with a seat for life) to set laws is, to say the least, problematic.

'An Appalling Irresponsibility'

I do not believe in the current fashion of mocking the House of Lords. Yet I do believe that there is an appalling irresponsibility at the heart of it. It is irresponsible because, although the House of Lords helps make laws which govern the lives of citizens, it has no means of accounting for these decisions in front of the same citizens. Power without responsibility, indeed! We can hardly encourage responsible citizenship—where citizens take responsibility for their actions—whilst such a poor example is set at the top.

Nor am I sure that the present system of creating life peerages promotes that much vaunted attribute, independence. Now of course no one would suggest that a good number of our modern life peers are placemen and women. Exactly the opposite. Many are indeed of independent mind and disposition. Yet they are not the norm. The sad fact is that the life peerage appointments procedure tends to promote, not independence of mind, but rather conformity. Essentially, party political leaders determine the composition of the modern peerage, and this gives them inordinate, if not corrupting, power. The reality is that all the pressures tend to force many of the aspirants to stay on the right side of his or her respective patron in order to be appointed.

What is more, there remains the question of the bishops and the judges. The presence of bishops and judges in our Upper House violates the basic liberal democratic principles obtaining in every other modern democracy—those of the separation of powers and separation of church and state. It is reasonable to ask: What are they doing there? Bishops should be in the church, not in a legislature! Judges should be in the courts, not in a law-making body!

All in all, the House of Lords—both as presently named and constituted—is in a false position in a modern polity. Of course, democratic imperatives do not demand that the House of Lords—any more than the monarchy—be abolished. These pre-democratic institutions, reflecting as they do part of our history, can become advisory and decorative bodies. Democratic imperatives do demand, however, that they should have no constitutional rôle. Looking to the future, it seems to me highly unlikely that, say, 30 years from now Britain will still possess the existing constitutional construct in which hereditary institutions like the monarchy and the House of Lords have a place in a democratic constitution.

4. Conclusions

In conclusion, therefore, radicals should—as radicals must—at least attempt to get 'to the root of the matter'. In the 1980s our most recent burst of radicalism made such an attempt—to confront, not dodge, our endemic economic problems. In my view, the 1990s, and beyond that the next millennium, should witness an attempt to confront our very constitution, to liberalise it, to modernise it—so that it begins to complement, rather than obstruct, our development as a modern nation.

4

THE POLITICAL ECONOMY
OF CABINET CHANGE*

Richard Rose

Director, Centre for the Study of Public Policy,
University of Strathclyde

Introduction

A CABINET MINISTER'S JOB is one of the most important positions in the British system of government. A Secretary of State is the link between the voice of the people as expressed in Parliament, and the mind of civil servants, as expressed in Whitehall. The public rôle of a Minister in Parliament and on television will never be overlooked. However, his rôle inside government is just as important: to give direction to departmental officials expert in dealing with problems there. A Minister who is unable to give this direction is simply a passenger on a ship of state that is adrift, or run on automatic pilot by the civil service.

The influence of Ministers within their departments is today challenged on many fronts. The Thatcher era provides examples of 10, Downing Street imposing main lines of policy from above. While this could be justified as an increase in political influence by the leader of the governing party, it incidentally undercut the authority of Ministers within their own departments. When the Prime Minister did not

---

*A revised version of a paper first published under the title 'Too Much Reshuffling of the Cabinet Pack?', *IEA Inquiry* No. 27, September 1991.

intervene—and no Prime Minister can or wants to deal with everything at once—their insecurity caused the very problem that Downing Street complained of.

The growth of government has exposed as a constitutional fiction the doctrine that a single Secretary of State is responsible for all that is done in a department. The average Whitehall department is now divided into about 25 different divisions, each accounting for tens or hundreds of millions of pounds—and many of these units are further subdivided. Each division and subdivision represents a specific and often technical area of responsibility remote from a Secretary of State.

The increasing influence of the European Community upon British policy has added a new dimension to the responsibilities of Ministers. Since the EC normally operates through councils of departmental Ministers, a Secretary of State for Transport or Agriculture or Energy must deal with opposite numbers in 11 other countries. A British representative who has spent only a few months or a year in the job is handicapped when negotiating with Continental Ministers who often hold their post for three or four years, or may have devoted their whole career to a subject which a British Minister has been landed with by a political accident.

Notwithstanding the complexity of each ministry, most Secretaries of State last only two years in a particular post, a time span far shorter than in industry, the church, universities or other major public bodies. Moreover, there is no evidence that the rate of turnover is slowing down.

The reshuffling of Cabinet Ministers is a commonplace of British politics. Yet to prescribe that Britain ought to be governed by the best men and women for the job begs the question: What is the job of a Cabinet Minister? More than one answer can be given. The first section sets forth evidence showing what the rate of turnover is, how it compares with that elsewhere, and it explains the political determinants of frequent reshuffling of the Cabinet pack. To answer the question: Is this desirable? we must be clear about what the job of a Cabinet Minister is and is not. A Cabinet Minister is first and foremost a departmental ambassador, representing its problems and achievements to the world outside, starting with Parliament. A Minister is not a maker of policies *per se*, for very few Ministers are experts in the work of departments. The paper considers a variety of possibilities for reform; it concludes that reform is best sought by the creation of policy directorates within departments, mixing ambassadorial Ministers and junior Ministers and expert civil servants.

TABLE 1

TURNOVER OF CABINET MINISTERS,* 1964-91

No.	Departments	Labour 1964-70 (6 Years)	Conservative 1970-74 (4 Years)	Labour 1974-79 (5 Years)	Conservative 1979-91 (12 Years)	Average
21	DTI	3+	3	3+	12	1·3
16	Transport	4	1	3	8	1·7
14	Employment	2	3	2	7	1·9
14	Environment	3	2	2	7	1·9
13	FCO	4	1	3	5	2·1
13	Educ. & Science	4	1	3	5	2·1
13	DHSS	4	1	2	6	2·1
(12)	Energy	—	(1)	2	5	2·2
12	Home Office	3	2	2	5	2·2
(12)	N. Ireland	—	(2)	2	5	2·2
10	MAFF	2	2	2	4	2·7
10	MOD	1	2	2	5	2·7
9	HM Treasury	2	2	1	4	3·0
8	Wales	3	1	1	3	3·4
7	Scotland	1	1	2	3	3·8
6	Lord Chancellor	1	1	1	3	4·7
6	Prime Minister	1	1	2	2	4·7
196	No. Ministers	38	26	35	89	
	No. Departments	16	15·5	17	18	18
	Average years in office	2·53	2·38	2·43	2·43	2·48

( ) Total number adjusted to represent full period since 1964.

 * Omits Cabinet posts solely concerned with political management.

1. How Much Turnover?

The British Record

The era of the full-time professional politician began when Harold Wilson, who spent his adult working life in Whitehall and Westminster, entered Downing Street in 1964. In the quarter-century since, control of government has alternated frequently between Conservatives and Labour, reflecting an electoral desire for change in the direction of public policy.

Changing the party in control of government does not require frequent reshuffles of the Cabinet pack. If every member of the Wilson

Cabinet appointed in 1964 had remained in office throughout Labour's hold on government, then each would have held the same job for almost six years. The duration of the Heath administration was less than four years, and five and one-half years for the Wilson-Callaghan government. Margaret Thatcher was unique in this century in longevity in office. However, no one except herself sat in Cabinet for a decade. Only three members of the Cabinet that she appointed in 1979 were still there after the 1987 election (Lord Whitelaw, Sir Geoffrey Howe and Peter Walker)—and none remains today.

The average length of time in which a politician is head of a Whitehall department is just under two and one-half years (Table 1). In the course of a four-year Parliament a department can expect to have two different Secretaries of State, and in a decade four different heads, whether or not there is a change in the government of the day.

Even though politicians today may feel more insecure—because of the threat of mass eviction by the electorate or because of loss of Prime Ministerial favour—there has been no tendency for Ministerial reshuffles to occur more frequently today than a quarter-century ago (Figure 1). Across eight Parliaments and six Prime Ministers, turnover occurs with the same frequency under Conservative and Labour governments. Turnover in the Conservative administration since 1979 has been at exactly the same rate as under its Labour predecessor and in the Heath administration, and only five weeks more frequent than under the 1964 Labour government.

Ministerial turnover differs far more between departments than between parties (Figure 2). The Trade and Industry departments have experienced the greatest changes, with 21 different Ministers in charge during the past 27 years. In part, this reflects frequent structural re-organisation, dividing responsibilities between two or more departments, and then merging them again into a single department. Margaret Thatcher initially had separate Cabinet Ministers for Trade and for Industry. Five different politicians held one or the other of these two offices. In June 1983 the departments were merged—and the rate of turnover increased. In the eight years since merger, seven different Ministers have been in charge of the DTI.

Rapid turnover is not confined to one department. Secretaries of State in Transport, Employment, and Environment have also held their post for less than two years on average. Seven more departments—the Foreign Office, Education, Health, Social Security, Energy, the Home Office and Northern Ireland—have normally had

Figure 1: Average Tenure of Ministers by
Governing Party, 1964-91

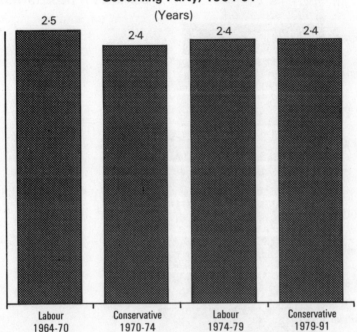

(Years)

their Minister leave shortly after celebrating a second anniversary in office.

Responsibility for handling large sums of money does not cause Ministers to be kept in place longer. The 11 departments that have an above-average rate of turnover in Ministers, such as Social Security, Education and Health, together account for more than four-fifths of public expenditure.

By contrast, the average Prime Minister spends twice as long in Downing Street as she or he allows a Minister to remain in a particular post. A push from the electorate or from the party is normally what it takes to reshuffle the Prime Minister.

Only two politically important departments—the Treasury and Defence—have had less than average rates of Ministerial turnover. Many of the posts with the least turnover, such as the Lord Chancellorship or the Secretary of State for Scotland or Wales—are normally out of the political limelight at Westminster. A shortage of Scots and Welsh MPs makes Conservative Prime Ministers hesitate to

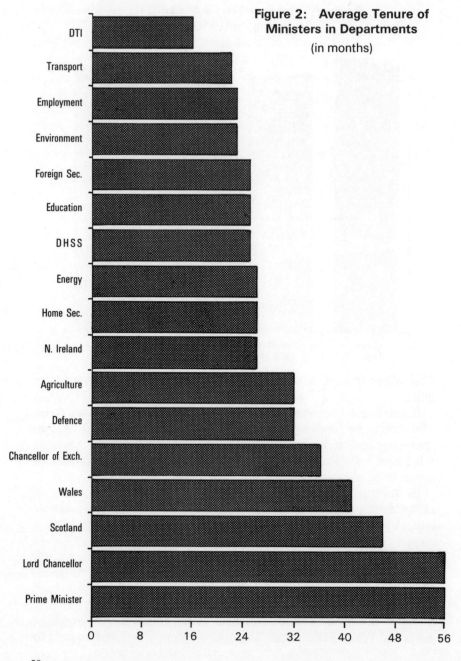

Figure 2: Average Tenure of Ministers in Departments (in months)

rotate incumbents, and Labour Prime Ministers have always looked for loyalty in Cabinet from long-term appointees there.

Disruption of Frequent Re-organisation

The figures shown for Cabinet turnover actually *under*state the turbulence of the typical Secretary of State's position. Ministries as well as Ministers have frequently been subject to re-organisation. Sometimes, this is no more than a 'repackaging' or change of label, adopted on symbolic grounds. But in fields such as trade and industry, re-organisation can involve the shift of programmes or personnel between departments.[1] A Minister placed in charge of a department that itself is a new mixture of programmes and people requires time before its different parts can coalesce.

Insofar as junior Ministers at the rank of Ministers of State and Parliamentary Under Secretaries are involved in the direction of a department, turnover at this level is a further disruption. Junior Ministers can be reshuffled independently of their Secretary of State, and a rapid flow of junior Ministers in and out is normal. Trade and Industry again provides an extreme example. Since 1979 it has had 12 Cabinet Ministers, 25 Ministers of State in charge of particular functional branches, and 20 Parliamentary Under Secretaries. Environment has had 18 Ministers of State and 25 Parliamentary Under Secretaries.

When a change occurs, an incoming Minister gets no time to prepare for the job, and normally no advice from his or her predecessor. When a person takes over a Cabinet post mid-term in a government, the new Minister is likely to be transferred from another department with no more than a spectator's knowledge of new responsibilities. If sacked from Cabinet, the outgoing Minister will not be regarded as a good source of advice, and if still in Cabinet will be considered a potential back-seat driver. When the Opposition takes over after an election, many new Ministers will have been shadowing the department for which they become responsible. However, the job of a shadow Minister is to oppose what government does, not understand it. Getting things right is harder than criticising what is wrong.

---

[1] See Richard Rose, *Ministers and Ministries*, Oxford: Oxford University Press, 1987, Chapter 2.

More Turnover Than Elsewhere?

By the standards of most leading positions in British society, the rate of turnover of Cabinet Ministers is very high. A managing director of a leading company would expect to spend half a dozen years in the post, and a bishop often remains in place for a decade or more. In universities, a professor may be a department head for only a few years, but each academic devotes 30 to 40 years to mastering a single field of knowledge.

Within Whitehall, the most relevant comparison is with turnover in the civil service. Cabinet Ministers differ in two fundamental respects from the civil servants who advise them. First, civil servants have a much greater knowledge of how Whitehall works. They have normally spent 20 to 30 years there before reaching a high post. Such experience gives civil servants great familiarity with how government departments conduct their affairs and respond to Ministerial initiatives, and excellent contacts in many departments.

Secretaries of State lack the civil servants' lengthy experience of Whitehall. This remains true when one party holds office for a lengthy period. The Conservative Cabinet in 1964 had skipped more than two political generations from the Cabinet that entered government in 1951. Over a period of 12 years Harold Wilson similarly ran through 'generations' of Cabinet Ministers. The uninterrupted tenure of Conservatives since 1979 has also seen a turnover of generations. In the present Conservative government a typical Secretary of State will have gained a junior governmental post in the early 1980s and a promotion in the mid-1980s, before finally entering Cabinet.

Second, Cabinet Ministers rarely know the specifics of departmental business as do civil servants. Many civil servants will have spent a decade or two within a single department, seeing its work from many different angles, and learning how its parts fit together. A few will have spent virtually their whole period within a single department, such as the Foreign Office, the Treasury or the Scottish or Welsh offices. A Minister may have been exposed to a limited extent to its work as a shadow spokesperson or a junior Minister, but this is introductory not specialist knowledge.

By comparison with European neighbours, British Ministers tend to show a relatively high rate of turnover in office (Figure 3). In Austria the average Minister holds a post for almost five years, and in Sweden and Germany almost four years. The lower rate of turnover there is a reminder that coalition government is not necessarily a cause of

Figure 3: Average Duration in Office of Cabinet Ministers in Europe, 1945-84
(Years)

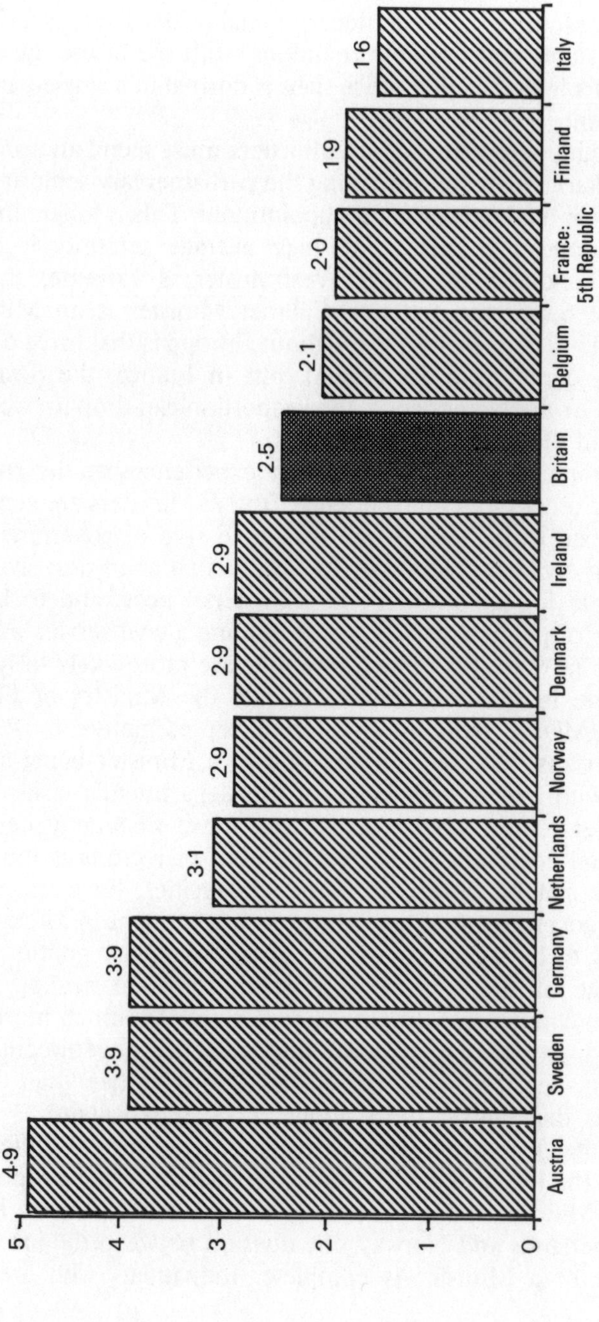

Source: Jean Blondel and Jean-Louis Thiebault (eds.), *The Profession of Government Ministers in Western Europe*, London: Sage Publications, 1991, p. 93. Average for the period 1945-1984.

frequent reshuffles between departmental posts. There is a distinction between stable and unstable coalitions, with the former guaranteeing Ministers a longer stay in office than is normal in a single-party British government.

In Britain, potential Cabinet Ministers must spend an average of 12 years in Parliament, accumulating the parliamentary seniority thought necessary as a qualification for appointment. This is longer than in any other European country. The high average seniority is linked to another condition in which Westminster is extreme; the almost invariable requirement that a Cabinet Minister is an MP prior to appointment. The average throughout Europe is that three out of four Ministers come from Parliament, but in France, the Scandinavian countries or the Netherlands, the proportion can drop to two-thirds or barely half (Figure 4).

The emphasis upon parliamentary experience has the corollary of devaluing other types of experience. British Ministers are very unlikely to have had experience in the executive side of government before becoming a Cabinet Minister. In Continental countries, civil servants are eligible for appointment to Ministerial posts and to be known members of political parties whilst holding a civil service post. Prime Ministers in the Fifth French Republic are more likely to have spent more time in the civil service, usually the Ministry of Finance or Foreign Affairs, than as an elected representative in Parliament. Scandinavians, too, see nothing odd in a Minister being an ex-civil servant with expert knowledge of the department's tasks.

Another reason why expertise can more frequently be found in continental governments is that the pool of recruits is much larger; Ministers can be drawn from the universities, business, unions or regional government. When Ministers are brought in as experts, they are likely to have less knowledge of parliamentary politics but more knowledge of the subject with which they are dealing. In every European country but Britain, Ministers are also much more likely to have had experience of local and regional government. This is important because it is these institutions rather than Whitehall ministries that deliver most public services in Britain.

In some European countries there is a formal differentiation between the job of the MP as a representative of the people, and the job of a Minister as the head of an executive department. In France, the Netherlands and Norway, the division between the job of an MP and that of a Minister is complete. Individuals who are MPs on

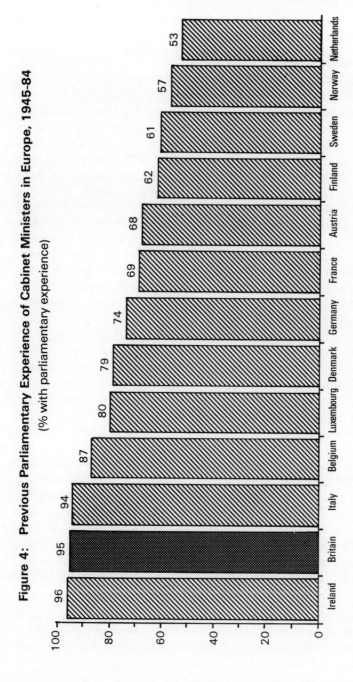

Figure 4: Previous Parliamentary Experience of Cabinet Ministers in Europe, 1945-84
(% with parliamentary experience)

Source: Jean Blondel and Jean-Louis Thiebault (eds.), *The Profession of Government Ministers in Western Europe*, London: Sage Publications, 1991, p. 48. Average for the period 1945-1984.

appointment are required to resign their parliamentary seat as a condition of taking Ministerial office.

Why So Much Turnover?

Three reasons account for the high degree of turnover in British government. First of all, a Ministerial job or promotion to a higher-status job at Westminster is the focus of political ambition. In becoming a Minister, the subject-matter of the department is of secondary significance. For a neophyte in the House of Commons, any department is a good one. At a later stage ambitious politicians may become more discriminating; some set their sights on the Foreign Office and others on the Treasury, or even Downing Street.

The longer a party is in office, the more important it is for an MP to serve an apprenticeship as a Parliamentary Under Secretary, and then as a Minister of State. Such jobs are not conceived as a training for a career, as is the civil service post of Principal. But the terms on which a junior Minister operates are, as Theakston notes, 'enfeebled' by the Secretary of State's individual responsibility for the department, and by the way in which the Secretary of State relies upon or excludes junior departmental Ministers.[2]

Reaching the top in Cabinet is like hill climbing; a straight line is rarely the best way up. Each step up in a Ministerial career is likely to be a diagonal movement between one department and another. It is often a condition of a Parliamentary Under Secretary rising to the rank of Minister of State that he or she moves to another department and takes up a totally new set of concerns.

Whereas a Minister is a politician in motion and hoping to move up, being Prime Minister is about staying put. Immediately, a Prime Minister is concerned with maintaining his or her position as party leader, and then with winning the next election. The end of Margaret Thatcher's period in office is a pointed reminder that managing the government party must come first. Harold Wilson never lost sight of that. He describes in a memoir how he carefully constructed his Cabinet to have up to six different rivals in it, as part of a game of 'musical daggers', in which rivals are intimidated against challenging the Prime Minister for fear that the hand that plunges the dagger in the leader will not inherit the prize of office.[3]

---

[2] For a detailed analysis of the disabilities of being a junior Minister, see Kevin Theakston, *Junior Ministers in British Government*, Oxford: Blackwell, 1987.

[3] Harold Wilson, *The Governance of Britain*, London: Sphere Books, 1977, pp. 52f.

A Prime Minister manages the governing party by using powers of appointment, or the promise of office. For this reason, Ministers can be chosen on grounds of personal loyalty (that is, rewarding friends), co-optation (bribing critics by giving them office and placing them under the constraint of collective Ministerial responsibility), or representativeness (a Scot, a woman, or a leader of a party group).

Competence in directing a specific government department (knowledge of foreign affairs, economic policy, health policy) is neither necessary nor sufficient for a Cabinet post. The need to win an election provides the strongest incentive for a Prime Minister to appoint competent Ministers, especially in such politically sensitive posts as the Treasury. It is no accident that the Chancellor is likely to have a longer tenure than most Cabinet Ministers, and more relevant experience in economic policy-making.

As circumstances change, a Prime Minister will reshuffle the Cabinet to give it a complexion in keeping with his or her political priorities, rewarding loyal and competent Ministers, and dismissing others. The prospect of a reshuffle is important in keeping Ministers and ambitious MPs in line. The Whips' Office uses the promise of office or the threat of exclusion as a means of enforcing support for the government's policy. Whips need not seek backbench support by stating the arguments for a given policy; they can point out the career consequences of opposing the leadership.

Chance and mortality also cause reshuffles. When Iain Macleod died a month after becoming Chancellor in 1970, Prime Minister Edward Heath was unexpectedly forced to fill a senior appointment. To minimise the impact upon the Cabinet, he appointed Anthony Barber. Similarly, when Foreign Secretary Anthony Crosland died less than a year after being appointed by a new Prime Minister, James Callaghan, the job was filled by Dr David Owen, who had been a Minister of State at the Foreign Office for only six months.

The politics of patronage can explain the frequency with which Ministers are moved from one department to another, but it does not prescribe what a Minister must do to be judged good by the standards of Westminster, and thus eligible for further promotion.

2. Consequences of Turnover

In parliamentary democracies, there are two different views of the job of a Cabinet Minister. One tradition, which Britain exemplifies, is that a Minister is first and foremost a politician, elected to Parliament to represent a party and its supporters in the electorate. From this perspective, being a Cabinet Minister is only an interlude in the life of an MP. Given that there are about eight times as many MPs as Ministerial appointments, this enables most MPs to be satisfied with their job as a representative. During a relatively brief period as a Minister, an MP's job is to represent party and parliamentary opinion to civil servants; in a nutshell, to tell civil servants what the public will not put up with.

An alternative is that a Minister is of central importance in giving direction to government. The Minister should be an expert executive, combining substantive knowledge of problems at hand with an understanding of the bureaucratic apparatus of government. The job of a Minister is thus defined as that of a leader of a large organisation, a task that has much in common with activities in many other institutions of society—but very different from that of being a Member of Parliament, which is perforce a 'free' rather than a bureaucratic job. Given the need for expertise and organisational skills, it follows that there is no reason why a Minister should be recruited from Parliament. It makes sense to promote a senior civil servant to the top job, or to bring in someone from outside Parliament to take charge of the billions that a government spends, and the millions employed in the public sector.

A country writing a new Constitution may choose which model is more appropriate. In a country with a long tradition of honouring parliamentary representation, such as Britain, the immediate issue is not whether MPs should be Ministers, but what the consequences are of recruiting Ministers from Parliament and then frequently reshuffling them from one job to another.

The Ambassadorial Role of Ministers

MPs are 'people' people; they are accustomed to observing what other people are thinking and doing, and relating what they say and do to the audience which they are addressing. An interest in other people is not just idle curiosity; it is also an instrumental skill that MPs cultivate as a means of influence and persuasion. Mobilising the support of others, whether organised groups, cliques in the Commons or a TV audience, is a major concern of MPs. So too is the capacity to anticipate how people will react to proposals for government action. An idea that may appear logical to a civil servant or an academic—say, removing tax subsidies for a portion of mortgage interest payments—can look like political suicide to a Housing Minister.

Given this outlook, it is not surprising that Ministers give prominence to their rôle as an ambassador, representing policies to people and groups outside the department. Within government, a Minister is the department's ambassador to the Cabinet; its endorsement is needed for the department's major policies and handling of controversial issues. A Minister also represents the department on Cabinet committees concerned with battles over jurisdictional turf, and negotiates its annual allocation of public expenditure.

A large amount of a Minister's time is spent in representing the department and his persona to Parliament. A Minister is regularly held accountable in Parliament, defending its actions from criticism and seeking to inspire the confidence of colleagues in what the department is doing. The ability to represent the department on television and in media briefings is of increasing importance, as a complement to or even a substitute for success in the House of Commons. A good performance in Parliament, in the media and in party meetings maintains the Prime Minister's and the governing party's confidence. A Minister must also represent the department in discussions with the myriad pressure groups that surround it. Secretaries of State are also increasingly involved in representing its interests in meetings of the European Community's Council of Ministers.

An experienced MP can be expected to be a good ambassador for a department inside Whitehall, in Parliament, in the media and on party platforms. If an MP is not, dismissal from Cabinet is the result.

The Policy Role

A Minister can be a persuasive ambassador without being a policy-maker, for a leader is a politician whom others will follow. The route taken need not be determined by the politician who leads the procession.

In dialogues with Cabinet colleagues, in the House of Commons or in briefings of lobby correspondents, a Minister can appear knowledgeable—but that is only because others often know little or nothing about the department's responsibilities. However, in discussions with civil servants, a Minister is normally an amateur, that is, someone who may have an interest in the department's work but no claim to expert knowledge.

A Minister is continuously talking about policy, but the policies being advocated are not necessarily of a Minister's making. Many Ministers prefer to be policy selectors, allowing civil servants to identify policies regarded as administratively practicable, and from this restricted menu selecting one that can win popularity and endorsement by the Cabinet. Much of a Minister's time is also spent reacting to events outside the department's control. When there is an urgent need to act, a Minister will turn to civil servants who know more about the problem.

A Minister usually has neither the time nor the training to resolve long-term problems. Time is in very short supply. A Minister must hit the ground running—but most Ministers are toddlers rather than veterans in the work of their department. A newly installed Minister can anticipate little more than two years in the job. The first months will be spent learning the ropes of the department, and opening cupboards to find what skeletons have been left behind by predecessors of the same or the opposition party. Once this is done, a Minister has a few months in which to fight battles for legislation and expenditure in the year ahead. Just when a Minister is beginning to get the feel of a department, anxiety rises. The optimist thinks of the prospects of promotion, and the pessimist worries that being left in the same department for more than two years may be a sign of the loss of Downing Street's favour.

Most Ministers are transient passers-by in their department, here today and gone tomorrow—to a better job or to political oblivion. Thus, they have strong incentives to concentrate on topics that promise short-term popularity.

However, the vast majority of problems facing departments are not easily resolved overnight, but manifestations of underlying structural difficulties. The primary education of children will not be transformed within the two-year period that is the normal tenure of a Secretary of State for Education. Nor will the deficiencies in the skills of the nation's labour force be eliminated in the short tenure of a Secretary of State for Employment. Getting to grips with the problems of Britain's trade and industry can hardly be dealt with in the 16-month period that the head of the DTI is in office.

It takes two or three years to analyse a complex substantive problem, negotiate with affected political interests, and secure the endorsement of the Prime Minister and Cabinet for legislation. It is sometimes possible to push a decision through more quickly, but the shambles of local government finance is a reminder of what happens when a Prime Minister acts quickly without full consideration of substantive and political problems.

The enactment of an Act of Parliament is only the beginning. It takes several years to implement most policies. It can take even longer for their full effects to be felt. For example, any training initiative for 16-year-old school-leavers will take up to five years to register in the adult labour force, and more than five-sixths of the labour force in the year 2000 will still show the effects of having started work without proper training. Policy-making, as the German sociologist Max Weber wrote, requires patience, for it is 'a strong and slow boring of hard boards'.[4]

In these circumstances, it is not surprising that industrialists, educators, doctors and local government officials argue that measures in their field are often based on inadequate understanding. The complaint goes deeper than partisan differences; it can be heard under Labour as well as Conservative governments. Even those who accept the goals of the government of the day often criticise as inadequate or ill-conceived the means adopted to achieve its goals. For pressure groups, a Minister's amateur standing is an ambiguous attribute. As long as the Minister is predisposed to agree with the group's advice, it is an asset, but if a Minister's outlook is unfriendly, then it is a source of friction.

Given that Ministers have much stronger political values than substantive knowledge of their department, willpower can substitute for knowledge. When willpower is directed at objectives that prove to be feasible, a Secretary of State can score a personal triumph. But when it is not, the result can be disastrous. In the absence of both expertise and willpower, a Cabinet Minister can add little to the departmental view of an issue, and may be criticised as a captive of civil servants.

3. Alternatives for Reform

Ministers are very good at doing what they do, and they cannot be expected to do what they are not trained to do. Ministers are good ambassadors for government departments, promoting and defending what others—inside their department, in local authorities, the private sector, or even in other countries—do in their name.

However, Ministers are not so good at giving direction to government. To be expert at steering the ship of state requires the

---

[4] 'Politics as a Vocation', in H. H. Gerth and C. Wright Mills (eds.), *From Max Weber*, London: Routledge, 1948, p. 128.

appointment of Ministers with greater expertise, a longer stay there to learn from experience, or both. To some extent, expertise can compensate for a short period of office, for people who are familiar with a subject are better qualified to move quickly than those who are not. Similarly, a longer stay in office can make a Minister more knowledgeable and committed to deal with longer-term issues. What are the alternative means by which either or both goals might be achieved?

1. *No inclination to give Ministers more time*

In logic a Prime Minister could resolve the difficulty by keeping Ministers in the same post longer, as is done in a number of European countries. Establishing two years as a minimum and three years as desirable for a Minister to hold a post, would not prevent the earlier dismissal of patent failures. It would also justify keeping a Minister good at a particular job in place for the whole of a Parliament. A general election would be the normal point at which a reshuffle occurred, rather than reshuffle talk being a frequent story in the media and in the corridors of Westminster.

In practice the Prime Minister of the day has good political reasons for frequent reshuffling, because reshuffles (or the hope of preferment) are intimately linked with the management of the majority party in the House of Commons. A Prime Minister who forgets that he or she depends upon the support of the electoral college of MPs risks being undermined by mutterings of MPs, or even, as Margaret Thatcher unintentionally demonstrated, by a secret ballot of the parliamentary party.

Moreover, a Prime Minister has no incentive to think about career planning for Ministers, since most junior Ministers will only reach Cabinet rank, if at all, under a different incumbent of Downing Street. For any change to be acceptable to a Prime Minister, it must pay off in terms of better government here and now.

2. *No hope of hiving off political business from Whitehall*

MPs have turned their backs on careers in public sector agencies that are actually responsible for delivering most of the goods and services for which Ministers nominally answer to the Commons, such as local government or the National Health Service.

The 'Next Steps' initiative offers an opportunity for Ministers to divest themselves further of concern with the everyday activities of civil servants, such as the administration of motor vehicle licences, the patent office, government research establishments, or HMSO. The intention is to increase efficiency by placing responsibility in public agencies outside Whitehall but within a policy and resources framework authorised by a Secretary of State.

In theory, Next Steps agencies are intended to combine the Minister's constitutional responsibility for giving policy direction with the civil servant's skills as an expert in administration and management. Implicit is the assumption that 'policy' can be separated from 'administration'. Whilst a clear distinction may be drawn between issuing motor vehicle licences and issuing a diplomatic ultimatum, there is no clear demarcation between policy and administration at the point at which it counts most, the everyday relationship between Ministers and higher civil servants. The areas initially chosen to launch the Next Steps programme were of low political concern, with little likelihood of friction, because they were of no political interest to Ministers.

However, when a problem arises unexpectedly, then even seemingly routine agencies can be of immediate political concern. For example, the disclosure that forensic evidence has been improperly presented in court raises questions of political concern about the hived-off forensic science service. The BCCI affair is a reminder that Ministers must be very careful about the actions of inspectors on whose judgement the public relies.

MPs have the right to question actions of government, and they expect to address their questions to Ministers. Both know that if the MP does not like the answer given, a question can be raised in the House. A prison escape, an air accident or the collapse of a bank will immediately raise questions in Parliament that a Secretary of State is expected to answer—even if executive responsibility for a problem is in the hands of others. This will remain true of actions for which Next Steps agencies are responsible, for neither a Secretary of State nor Parliament wants to surrender Ministerial accountability.

A recent Efficiency Unit review, *Making the Most of Next Steps*, speaks delicately of the need to 'reconcile several interests'. In keeping with the 'saving of candle ends' origins of the programme, the Treasury's interest is put first, delivering services more cheaply. Ministers, and heads of the new agencies, also have interests. The dilemma inherent in the Next Steps approach is that the experts named as chief executives are expected to be publicly responsible for what is done, yet not to protest publicly as and when a Minister issues a policy directive with which they disagree, or the Treasury denies resources that they believe are necessary. The emerging friction between TECs and the Secretary of State for Employment is an example of the difficulty that Whitehall has in delegating tasks.

There are limits to what can be hived off without turning the public sector into a battlefield between agency heads and Ministers disputing who is responsible when problems arise. Furthermore, issues of major political concern—and every department has some, otherwise it would not achieve Cabinet rank—cannot be hived off. What can be done with these departments, the most important in government?

3. *How could more expertise be gained?*

One way to increase expertise is to change the criteria for appointing people to Ministerial posts. Present conventions create an extremely small (and, critics would add, shallow) pool, confined to a couple of hundred MPs who are not disqualified for promotion from the back-benches on political or personal grounds. There are two directions in which a Prime Minister looking for talent could turn: to the world outside Westminster, or to civil servants already inside Whitehall.

(a) *Importing outside experts who are amateurs in government?*

A career open to talents is the ideal of a democracy, but many occupations have restrictive qualifications for entry, and the Cabinet is no exception. Out of a pool of 13,700,000 persons who vote for the government of the day, the 300-odd eligible for a Ministerial post because they are MPs is 0·002 per cent of government supporters.[5]

Recruiting the best person for Cabinet, regardless of parliamentary career or party, is often prescribed by those without experience of government. The theory is that a person who is successful in business or academic work or trade unions will be equally successful as a Cabinet Minister. This prescription places a high value upon undefined personality traits of 'leadership'. It dismisses as of no importance the professional politician's skills.

If knowledge of a subject is deemed important, then it follows that experts could be recruited from outside Westminster—for example,

---

[5] The House of Lords can augment the ranks of Ministers but the Commons could not be expected to tolerate more than one or two departmental Ministers in the Lords, and even less tolerate parachuting a large number of new Ministerial appointees into the Lords or a large number of Ministers from outside Westminster.

businessmen at Trade & Industry, trade unionists at Labour, an educator at Education, and so forth. American Presidents tend to follow this pattern in recruiting their Cabinets. In Washington, as in a number of continental European countries, the recruitment of experts is often linked to the propitiation of pressure groups; for example, a representative of agricultural interests will be 'given' the Department of Agriculture, and a trade union spokesperson can be 'given' the Labour Department.

From time to time a Prime Minister has brought into government a person experienced in a department's field, but an amateur at Westminster. Frank Cousins moved from being head of Britain's largest union to Minister of Technology in the 1964 Labour government, and John Davies moved from the Confederation of British Industries to become Secretary for Trade and Industry. Cousins's union experience led Harold Wilson to hope that Cousins would mobilise support for Labour policies to 'revitalise' British industry. Davies's subject-matter expertise was intended to reflect Ted Heath's managerial promise of 'a new style of government'. By common consent, neither was a success.

Outsiders normally fail because they are amateurs as political ambassadors representing a department within Whitehall, in Parliament and to the public. A Minister will be held in low esteem if he or she does not know how to get the better of an Opposition MP seeking to rise by doing the Minister down. A Minister inexperienced in Cabinet committees or in the ways of civil servants will also come out badly in the jungle warfare of Whitehall. Importing Ministers from outside is unlikely to be successful.

(b) *Promote experienced civil servants to Ministerial rank?*

The irony of Ministerial direction of the civil service is that it assumes that a large and experienced cadre of men and women recruited as the 'best and the brightest' to manage government departments can be directed by amateurs in the work of the departments.

A civil service career normally involves a working lifetime in Whitehall. Competition within the civil service is muted but real. To rise to a high position in Whitehall a civil servant must be good at working the complex machinery of government, in all its departmental, interdepartmental and procedural complexity, including arcane features that arise because public administration is neither private enterprise nor even, at times, common sense. This knowledge is highly specialised, and is at the core of a civil servant's claim to professional expertise.

In addition, civil servants are experienced at watching and managing Ministers, learning when enthusiasm must be real and not feigned; when to say 'Yes, Minister', when they mean 'perhaps'; and 'Not quite, Minister', when they mean 'No'. A publication of the First Division Association promises bright graduates:

> 'You will be involved from the outset in matters of major policy or resource allocation and, under the guidance of experienced administrators, encouraged to put forward your own constructive ideas and to take responsible decisions.'[6]

A third asset of senior civil servants is that they have specialist knowledge about the work of particular departments. Almost half have had their careers concentrated in one or two departments, and it is abnormal for an official to rotate among more than four departments in a career of almost 40 years. A senior civil servant is likely to have spent a decade or two concentrating on what happens within a department, as against the few years of intermittent attention that a new Minister may have given from a less-favoured vantage point as a shadow spokesperson or junior Minister.

Higher civil servants suffer from the vice of their virtues. Precisely because of spending a working life in Whitehall, they are often unfamiliar with the world outside it. This includes ignorance of the way in which local government services and the health service work, as well as of the private sector. The experience of seeing fresh ideas lead to political disaster makes civil servants sceptical, and cautious. They are good at defending the *status quo* as a lesser evil than any proposal for change.

Civil servants also lack experience of being a public ambassador for public policy. All their efforts are behind the scenes, as part of the private government of public policy. Civil servants do not want to be out front; they have a passion for anonymity rather than the passion for publicity that drives their university contemporaries into politics, the media, advertising or other fields where success is tested publicly rather than by activities that are official secrets.

Ministers are prepared to share the work of Whitehall with civil servants—as long as they are not competitors. The understanding is

---

[6] *Careers in the Civil Service—An Alternative View*, London: First Division Association, 1987, p. 12.

that the Minister will take credit for all the successes that the department can boast, even when they are the achievements of a team of civil servants, and carry the burden of defending the department from criticism of mistakes that are not the Minister's personal fault.

Any proposal to appoint civil servants instead of Ministers to Cabinet posts would be strongly opposed by those who have most to lose, MPs. The fact that it is done in other countries, including the United States, is not an answer. MPs are not competing to become Ministers in Paris or Washington; the prize they seek is in Whitehall.

4. *Combining skills in a policy directorate*

The tasks of Ministers and civil servants are not antagonistic but complementary; both are needed to steer the ship of state.[7] The challenge is to integrate better the skills of Ministers as ambassadors and civil servants as experts. There is a need to temper the enthusiasms of Ministers with a recognition of obstacles, and to 'heat up' civil servants so that they become more committed to find means of setting right what has patently gone wrong.

At present, a ministry is a curious dyarchy, in which the Secretary of State is at the top of a pyramid without a base, and the Permanent Under Secretary is supported by a mass of civil servants, but is not on top. Ministers and civil servants deal with each other regularly, but civil servants are always *ir*responsible, that is, what they do is done in the name of the Minister. Often, the Secretary of State is uninformed, because there is never time to monitor all that happens within a department and lack of knowledge makes it difficult for a Minister to anticipate what is going right or wrong.

The creation of a *policy directorate* would end this division by bringing together a dozen or so MPs, civil servants and, if appropriate, outside experts, with immediate responsibility for tasks of concern to the Secretary of State. Within this group there would be individuals, usually civil servants, overseeing broad blocks of departmental work, and individuals concerned with *ad hoc* matters, such as a bill going through Parliament, normally an MP. There would be at least one MP with a particular concern for mobilising political support for the department, and at least one person concerned with longer-term departmental problems. Crisis problems could be assigned to the person most suited

---

[7] See Richard Rose, 'Steering the Ship of State: One Tiller but Two Pairs of Hands', *British Journal of Political Science*, Vol. 17, 1987, pp. 409-33.

to the needs of the moment. The policy directorate would combine tasks and people that are currently divided between Ministers of State, Parliamentary Under-Secretaries and civil servants.

Logic of a Policy Directorate

The logic of a policy directorate is to bring together in a single team people who are professional ambassadors with those who are professional experts. Members of the directorate would be in operational charge of the department; it would thus be different from an advisory or personal support group, like the French *Cabinet* system. The Washington concept of having a department head as Mr or Ms Outside, acting as an ambassador to Congress, the White House and the media, and a Mr or Ms Inside, giving direction to the department, captures the intention here. A Secretary of State would retain separately assistants, devoted to furthering his or her political standing in the party and in the media. The department would have an Administrative Secretary who could look after housekeeping matters of no interest to a transient Minister.

The Secretary of State's accountability to Parliament would not be diminished by the creation of a policy directorate, for he or she would still have to answer in public for what the department did, and to act as an ambassador within Whitehall, too. What would change is the relationship between the Minister and the department. As the chair of the policy directorate, a Secretary of State would be in a position to monitor what was being done in his or her name, and to determine major lines of policy. Senior and expert staff within the directorate would report directly to the Secretary of State, rather than through a Permanent Under Secretary whose job would become more oriented towards departmental administration. MPs serving in the policy directorate would have more authority *vis-à-vis* civil servants than at present, yet still remain answerable to the Secretary of State.

Recruitment of the policy directorate should be a joint enterprise, starting in Downing Street. Greater consultation between Downing Street and Ministers about junior appointments would be desirable, but the last word must remain with the Prime Minister, whose job it is to manage Secretaries of State as well as the party. Civil servants could be offered posts in the policy directorate or volunteer for a task that could be risky in conventional civil service terms. A civil servant out of sympathy with the priorities of a policy directorate could refuse a post. If a number refused to back a particular panacea of the moment, this information would be a tacit vote of no confidence by administrators, a warning but not a veto of action. Outside experts would be hired for specific positions; their appointment would expire when their job was done or the task abandoned. A policy directorate of 15 people might have three MPs in addition to the Secretary of State, about 10 civil servants and two outside experts.

Evolutionary Change

Change could be introduced in an evolutionary manner. The Treasury and the Foreign & Commonwealth Office are two places to start. Both departments are of the highest importance—to the country as well as to the Prime Minister and the party in government. Each is full of career civil servants who are expert in their field. Collectively, each department's experts reflect a wide range of opinions. The Treasury is neither a monetarist nor a Keynesian monolith. Experts in both departments already have a degree of visibility to the *cognoscenti* outside Whitehall. What they lack is the authority to press a case hard within their department. A policy directorate would offer opportunities to talent—and high rewards to those who succeeded. If the experiment there were successful, it could spread to other departments. For example, given an absolute shortage of MPs in Scotland and Wales, a Conservative government might welcome an opportunity to recruit more widely for the Scottish and Welsh offices.

The resulting changes would not upset the Secretary of State's accountability for what the department does. He or she would continue to answer in Whitehall, in Parliament, in the party, and in the media. But it would encourage the Secretary of State to abandon the constitutional fiction that one person does everything in a department, and speak more often in terms of 'We'. A Minister could use members of the policy directorate to stake out controversial positions in advance of a personal commitment. Recognition that the Secretary of State is not doing everything within a department would also make it possible to deal at arm's length with Next Steps agencies.

Junior Ministers would have a clearer choice of rôles than at present; either they could concentrate upon supporting the Secretary of State *qua* ambassador, or take responsibility for a specific policy area or issue within the department. A Secretary of State would welcome having an MP as a Political Secretary and another as a Political Under-Secretary to deputise as his representative. In the Treasury, the Chief Secretary would as now be responsible for a functional task, public expenditure. In a ministry such as Education, responsibility for primary and secondary schools could be given to people who actually knew something about their work—not least recruits from outside Whitehall—rather than to transient MPs. Since the experts would remain accountable to politicians, they would only take the job if satisfied that what was expected was consistent with their own values, and with what was practicable.

The great majority of high-ranking civil servants would continue as before, toiling away from the limelight, doing work that was not of political interest. Their pay and conditions, including anonymity, would remain as before.

Individual Responsibility and Initiative

The very small number of civil servants introduced to the policy directorate would face a major sea change. They would report directly to the Secretary of State, rather than working through junior Ministers (who could veto or misunderstand their views), or through very senior civil servants who could act as a brake upon individual initiative. Public identification with a policy would make a civil servant cautious about advocating a policy just because it was a popular nostrum in the governing party, for if it failed, his or her career would suffer. This would be a major brake upon the adoption of half-baked ideas. If a new initiative succeeded, a civil servant would share in the credit. Positions in the policy directorate would appeal to civil servants with initiative and ideas congenial, or at least, not unacceptable, to the political values of the governing party. They would not appeal to civil servants who do not like to take individual responsibility.

Because the world of Whitehall is a small one, it would be easy enough to identify civil servants well suited to serve in a policy directorate. But what happens when a civil servant has finished a tour of duty in a policy directorate? The numbers involved are small. Even if all appointments lapsed at the end of a Parliament, more than 90 per cent of higher civil servants would remain unaffected. Some leaving policy directorates would be of retirement age; for such veterans, this age could be lowered to 55. Involvement in the political work of a policy directorate should not be a barrier to another civil service job at the same or higher rank and salary. After all, Whitehall sees nothing odd in a civil servant being the Private Secretary to a Conservative and then a Labour Prime Minister, returning to the Treasury and ending up as Head of the Home Civil Service (e.g. Sir Robin Butler).

The offer of a chance to do something in their own right, rather than as a puppet master, should encourage more creative civil servants to come forward with fresh ideas more readily. Success in a policy directorate would give a civil servant a wide choice of options—to return to a higher post in Whitehall, to leave Whitehall in order to pursue the same idea from outside central government, or to turn to another type of job.[8] Washington provides an example of extremely able civil servants leaving government after 20 years, the minimum required for a pension, and turning their hand to other activities. A civil servant in his or her forties might welcome the fresh stimulus of a change of job, not to mention the higher salary. In turn, this would open opportunities for promoting younger civil servants. In an era in which everyone from corporate executives to Catholic seminarians need not regard an initial job as a permanent career, there is much to be said for the opportunity to change careers.

MPs would still be able to interrogate the Secretary of State about everything that went on within a department, and to lobby him privately, or discuss issues with MPs who were part of the policy directorate. Civil servants in the policy directorate would not only appear before committees of the House but also be expected to defend policies for which they were responsible, rather than hide behind the fig leaf of the Secretary of State's intentions. This would be good for the committees, and the heat would also make civil servants more individually responsible.

Broad Political Objectives

Insofar as the Prime Minister is interested in more effective government, creating policy directorates would be an advantage, mobilising more expert advice in the service of the broad political objectives of the governing party. Appointments to the policy directorate would not only be matters of party and of civil service patronage but also issues of political priorities. Does a particular post in a policy directorate require an individual who can mobilise political support for an issue (an MP) or an expert who can see through technical obstacles to a change of policy (an outsider with specialist knowledge) or someone to negotiate a complicated re-organisation of the delivery of a government service (a veteran civil servant)?

---

[8] See 'The Attractions of Exit', in Richard Rose, *Loyalty, Voice or Exit? Margaret Thatcher's Challenge to the Civil Service*, Glasgow: Strathclyde Studies in Public Policy No. 166, 1988.

A mixed policy directorate offers a Prime Minister, the Secretary of State and the Head of the Civil Service a chance to approach appointments on a horses-for-courses basis. The number of Cabinet posts would remain unaffected, thus leaving the Prime Minister with the same number of senior posts for co-opting rivals and critics. The number of junior posts might decline slightly. If Whips found this made backbench MPs more unruly, then the Whips Office might be asked to find some other means of disciplining MPs than letting them 'practice' governing by being Parliamentary Under Secretaries.

Policy directorates within departments would avoid the problems of creating an alternative source of departmental policy-making in Downing Street. Keeping out of trouble is the second law of politics. Making decisions without knowing what you are talking about is a sure way of getting into trouble. With a policy unit of less than a dozen, Downing Street cannot be staffed to take informed decisions on all major departmental issues. The creation of larger staff, on the model of the German Chancellor's office or the White House, would lead only to endless second-guessing, in which a Prime Minister would be pulled into rows with Ministers on issues selected by staff, and not by the Prime Minister.

The most effective way for a Prime Minister to influence policy without being drawn into departmental quarrels is through the appointment of Secretaries of State and key members of a policy directorate. Keeping policy in the departments keeps it close to expertise; it also distances Downing Street from the inevitable mistakes that will occur.

Strengthening the political direction of public policy by integrating partisans with political goals and experts with knowledge should increase democratic accountability, for the people in charge will collectively be better able to understand what government is and can do. Since giving direction to government is a complex task, it cannot be done solely by Ministers, or solely by civil servants. The ship of state has only one tiller, but there is a need for two pairs of hands.

5

GOVERNMENT BY CONTRACT*

Graham Mather
General Director,
Institute of Economic Affairs

Introduction

How should public services best be provided? To what extent can the disciplines of the market, captured through the processes of contractual relationships and competitive tendering procedures, invade the realms of Whitehall?[1]

To address these questions raises broader issues of the definition of public goods and the precise border between market and state. It also raises questions of the efficiency and legitimacy of redistributive techniques in securing desired policy outcomes. These subjects are beyond the scope of this paper, which is concerned with the scope for using explicit *contracts* within government. The paper suggests that regarding government service provision as a series of contracts presents new opportunities to improve service standards, set explicit performance standards, and improve customer entitlements or 'empowerment'. This contract system has several dimensions: contracts between those who specify and finance public services, and those who

*This chapter is a revised version of the paper first published as *IEA Inquiry* No. 25 in March 1991. Earlier versions were given as papers to the Royal Institute of Public Administration in September 1988 and to the Fabian Society in January 1991.

[1] Robert Skidelsky, *The Social Market Economy*, Social Market Foundation, 1989.

provide them, imposing effective quality control on and incentives for service providers; and contracts between providers and customers, whereby users of public services become entitled to defined performance standards and effective rights of redress.

End of Traditional Public Service

Since the middle of the 19th century, the concept of a benign public administration has been seen as an indispensable attribute of the state in helping government modify the outcomes of market processes. However, it is increasingly apparent that the objectives of government will not be secured by the traditional techniques of public service. Nor need they be. For example, neither basic protection against catastrophic loss of earning power nor the establishment of a framework for personal advance need depend upon the techniques of traditional public administration.

We will not secure the goals of government by building a handbook for enlightened administrators within the existing framework of government service provision. Equipped with the latest handbook, those administrators would undoubtedly do better in avoiding the more obvious government failures of the recent past, including nationalisation, state monopoly of unpriced but cash-limited health and welfare, dependency and over-ambitious estimations of the capabilities of central and local government and their agencies. However, in an unchanged framework there is no reason to expect that cash-limited, centrally-administered systems will do other than continue to defeat expectations. They promise too much and deliver too little.

The risk is of two simultaneous effects. First, placing new administrative burdens on government without new constraints risks moral hazard, regulatory overload, unquantified costs and crowding-out effects. Secondly, the hands of enlightened administrators end up guided by vote motives, yielding to the demands of organised interest groups.

Public agents do not benefit from the superior discovery procedure of the market: they do not face the sort of incentives that lead economic agents to exploit market opportunities, reduce costs and research new ways of producing or delivering goods and services. Public agents are not subject to the objective criteria of the market; their self-interest is not dependent upon them being able to increase sales, reduce costs and increase profitability. Instead they are subject to administrative or political discretion; able to make decisions with little regard to considerations of cost, efficiency or customer satisfaction. The absence of market information means that public agents can only act upon their own perceptions of what the recipients of their services might want or what they find most rewarding or convenient; if not, the only external criteria they can act upon are the crude measures of customer surveys or the dictates of politicians.

The main problem that public agents face is a lack of quality information. It is not that the information does not exist or that public agents are so starved of funds that they cannot obtain that information. The problem is that public processes cannot possibly supply that information in the form of prices.

Empowerment and Classlessness

The challenge today is how to transform under-performing public services and align them with the methods of the market. The encouraging sign is that both left and right are now vigorously engaged in the search for techniques to achieve this: to empower people.

So there is a new consensus of objectives in British politics. It is to give individuals meaningful rights and entitlements that are real and enforceable. To put flesh on the bones of this concept of an open society is the biggest single challenge facing political thinkers during the 1990s.

The concept of empowerment can be developed in terms of classlessness. The idea of a classless Britain has led to a rather confused debate, with the emphasis on *social* class. Although this is revealing in itself, it is not, however, in this cultural sense that we should examine the concept.

Outdated 'class' attitudes are relevant primarily insofar as they perpetuate a dependent, deferential, uncomplaining culture in which citizens perceive poor service, oppressive or less than competent bureaucracy, lack of choice, scruffy and underperforming public services as somehow pre-ordained.

The most worrying 'class' attitudes are those which entrench this type of servile society. There is a clear escape route from this dependent relationship which passes through empowerment of people as customers of public services, with entitlements and choices, to opportunity to broaden the realm of choice in a working and competitive market economy.

Britain will only move away from being a servile society to become a more open, dynamic opportunity society if the public institutions which tend to sustain the servile society are reformed. Improved accountability and better public services can be achieved if a three-fold reform agenda is pursued.

1. *Achieving an Open Society*

The first is to approach questions of constitutional and institutional reform with an open mind, and with especial attention to the effective functioning of Parliament, open access to government information, and the codification of protection of individual rights.

Britain's constitutional and institutional structure has depended upon radical advance: on a radical concept of Parliamentary sovereignty, a radical Bill of Rights, radical reforms to suffrage. These democratic advances were not achieved by the assertion that former practices were immutable, or that 'something would turn up' to allow society to move forward without the need to think through the options and choices.

In the same way, it serves no advantage to assert that today's ways of running government, financing it, administering local services, providing information to citizens are by some marvellous chance the best of all possible worlds, relevant for yesterday, today and tomorrow without change or re-examination.

To entrench that sort of '*status quo* society' would be a profound disservice. The breath of fresh air which has transformed the shape of so much of business and commercial life, and removed the 'them and us' mentality which bedevilled industrial relations in the 1970s, can do the same in the areas under Whitehall's sway, where stuffy paternalism tends still to set the agenda.

2. *Government by Contract*

The second key opportunity is to change the nature of government so that it rests explicitly on a series of *contracts*, in the same way that contracts at base govern the rest of national life. Instead of administering public service, civil servants should begin explicitly to meet the requirements of customers. Services should be specified in clear, contractual terms; private providers given the opportunity to compete with Departments for their provision; and customers given clear contractual rights in terms of performance standards and rights of redress.

Of course, defining more clearly the expectations of customers of public services—local authority housing tenants, NHS patients, customers of monopolies like British Rail or regulated near-monopolies like British Telecom, users of government agencies like the Passport Office or Companies House—does not in itself close the broader discussions on the balance of public and private provision, or the nature of a 'fair' or 'opportunity' society. But by employing the same techniques which apply in relationships outside the public sector it makes these relationships more precise, explicit and transparent, and helps to make them more amenable to competition and choice.

3. *Empowerment*

Thirdly, citizens must have real decision-making power. And that power must be the result of a new model of government—government by contract, with contracts giving individuals real enforceable rights. Past models of open government have tended to rely on committees everywhere. The Left in particular has invested much intellectual capital in techniques of supposed participation through pseudo-democratic structures, quangos and representative bodies. They have failed the test. We should not be afraid to hand back government power to individuals by contracting with them, in a new social contract which is built up of millions of enforceable micro-contracts for better standards of public service. This may properly be provided through private contractors where they can do it best.

Future Trends in Government Scale and Organisation

Since publication of the Efficiency Unit's 1988 study, *Improving Management in Government: the Next Steps*,[2] there have been signs that a profound change has been under way concerning the manner through which government provides services and conducts its relationships with the private sector. *Next Steps* had as its central recommendation that 'agencies should be established to carry out the executive functions of government within a policy and resources framework set by a department'.

As the Treasury and Civil Service Select Committee said in its report on *Next Steps*:[3]

---

[2] By Kate Jenkins, Karen Caines and Andrew Jackson, London: HMSO, 1988.

[3] Treasury and Civil Service Committee, Eighth Report: *Civil Service Management Reform: The Next Steps*, Vol. I: *Report, together with Proceedings of the Committee*, House of Commons Paper 494-I, London: HMSO, 1988, p. vi.

'As up to 95 per cent of the Civil Service is concerned with the delivery of services, this change could be the most far-reaching since the Northcote-Trevelyan reforms in the nineteenth century. If it proved possible to improve the effectiveness of such an overwhelming proportion of government business, this clearly would be of great national benefit.'

Yet a warning was set out by Sir Peter Middleton in his evidence from the Treasury. If the agency's objectives are not clearly established against real competitive and incentive pressures, as he said:

'You know, if you play the numbers game you can easily tot up a large number [of agencies] simply by changing names.'[4]

The lesson of attempts to control nationalised industries suggests that management will develop policy objectives of their own. They will not in practice leave policy to Ministers, and day-to-day administration to themselves. Nor, if the experience of the NHS Management Board is concerned, will Ministers easily renounce close involvement in the detail of service delivery, where this is politically sensitive.

The weakness of the agency approach is, therefore, that it is likely to lead to imprecise framework agreements between departments and agencies, which leave a significant degree of administrative discretion to departments. In addition, and in part because of this, agencies are sheltered from real market competition. Unlike their counterparts in local government, they lack precise service specifications which can be put to open competitive tender and tested against the bids of private providers.

The point was highlighted in a CBI task force study:[5]

'The Efficiency Unit has recommended that central Government departments responsible for delivering services be operated as "Agencies". While this may lead to some improvement, it will not yield the full benefit of opening them up to competition. Competitive tendering for the opportunity to carry out these functions is clearly the best option, and only in the unlikely event that this proves impracticable should the Agency system be used, under which they necessarily remain under Treasury control.'

One way to tackle this in future would be to establish a ranking hierarchy of preferences and institutionalise it.

---

[4] Treasury and Civil Service Committee, Session 1987-88, Eighth Report: *Civil Service Management Reform: The Next Steps*, Vol. II: *Annexes, Minutes of Evidence and Appendices*, House of Commons Paper 494-II, London: HMSO, 1988, p. 75, col. 2.

[5] *The Competitive Advantage*, London: CBI, October 1988, p. 10.

○ In future, before establishment of a 'Next Steps' agency, the function itself could be considered for full privatisation. Independent outside advice from management consultants should be an integral part of the review process before ministerial decisions are taken.

○ A second stage should be to draw up a specification for competitive tender for the provision of an agency service, for which existing private sector operators could bid.

○ Where this failed, it might be possible for management itself to launch a buy-out of the service. Only after reviewing these options does it seem to make sense to establish an executive agency. At that point, the terms and specifications of its function are critical. For it offers the opportunity for policy-makers themselves to review the aims which they seek to achieve, the performance measures they wish to apply, the quality and quantity of various aspects of the service, before going ahead. Otherwise, they might just as well change the name of that part of their Department, prepare for some difficulties in pay structure, tensions between policy-making and administrative initiatives coming both ways, and play the numbers game.

○ Existing agencies, too, could be re-examined in a systematic programme and exposed to competitive tender. There is no reason why existing agencies[6] should not be tested against open competition. A programme should be established to expose all existing agencies to a competitive tender process within the next five years.

As Sir John Cuckney put it in his evidence to the Select Committee:

'The problem of Ministerial overload seems to me to be a self-imposed problem caused by lack of selectivity and failure to establish priorities. . . . I see little hope for agencies being able to operate effectively unless they are free standing and operate with a trading fund. I do not believe it to be realistic for them to attempt to operate within a department especially if that department itself attempts to operate a matrix style of management and control.'[7]

---

[6] Listed in Appendix 1 (below, pp. 90-91). Other activities which are being considered for agency status are listed in Appendix 2 (below, pp. 92-93).

[7] House of Commons Paper 494-II, *supra.*, p. 118.

Yet there is an opportunity to square the circle. In the Treasury's rather more radical predecessor document to the *Next Steps*, departments were told:

'Departments should review *all* their activities to see if they offer scope for contracting out. There will be some activities close to the heart of the Department over which management will want to retain direct control, particularly where it is essential that there should be no possibility of a divergence of interests. But they need to think in each case whether the degree of trust, confidentiality or responsibility for taking decisions on the Minister's behalf makes it essential to keep the function in-house'[8] (emphasis in original).

The multi-departmental reporting team added:

'In our opinion these principles, adjusted as necessary to suit their different circumstances, could be applied also in the national health service, in local government and in non-departmental public bodies.' (p. 12)

These principles are already beginning to determine important relationships between local government and the private sector in local government and the NHS. They could easily be employed to take the next steps beyond Next Steps.

Drawing the Dividing Line Between Public and Private Provision

In central and local government, the dividing line between direct provision, and private provision of public services, is much closer to the core of government than has been imagined.

The government of Britain is moving towards a series of contracts, in which a core of fewer than 10,000 civil servants will specify and buy public services from outside agencies, private contractors and consortia of former public sector managers. Central government will be able to choose among competing suppliers of services formerly provided by itself or by local authorities, and gear its grants to results. With the exception of the armed forces, police and security services—which exercise direct power over the liberty of individual citizens—it is difficult to suggest that there *is* a dividing line between services which could be contracted out and those which must remain in government:

---

[8] *Using Private Enterprise in Government*, Report of a multi-departmental review of competitive tendering and contracting for services in government departments, HM Treasury, London: HMSO, 1986, p. 7.

o The divide is not departmental. There are activities in all departments of central and local government which can be contracted out.

o The divide is not commercial. Administrative as well as business functions can be carried out by staff not directly employed by the public sector, but working to a government remit.

o The divide is not between those who deal with the public, and backroom staff.

o And, as the use of car clamp contractors has shown, and in the discussions about private operation of prisons, it can come close to the exercise of functions affecting individual rights.

o If the division comes around the armed forces, it clearly does not exclude contracted ancillary staff; and British officers and men have contemporary experience of working on contract within overseas armed services, albeit generally as individuals.

Dividing between the rôles of public and voluntary sectors is equally difficult. These relationships will create particularly testing challenges as the voluntary sector seeks to fulfil a number of functions in its relations with the state, from wholly independent provision, to a catalytic and exhortatory rôle, through structured partnerships to direct provision on behalf of the state.

It is all the more encouraging, therefore, that a National Council for Voluntary Organisations/Royal Institute of Public Administration study[9] attached particular importance to the rôle of contracts. Its comments make a lot of sense:

'Public authorities and voluntary organisations need to get together to define good practice in the related fields of accountability, value for money review, and evaluation. Clear contracts, with both sides understanding what was to be expected, were for some participants the best safeguard. While voluntary organisations are often accused of vagueness and can be rather precious about their objectives, it is often the public authority which is hazy as to why it is funding a particular organisation. . . . Clarity about the nature of a contract and where it begins and ends should . . . allow voluntary organisations to own their own souls, even if parts of their bodies were for hire.'

---

[9] *Into the 1990s: Voluntary Organisations and the Public Sector*, NCVO/RIPA, 1988, p. 22.

Once again, putting government relations in terms of a contract can overcome perceived problems.

Of fundamental importance are the incentives and opportunities for public servants which the contractual approach opens up. The British model of public service tends to foster job security at the expense of market pay and other conditions. The contract model is exciting not least because it holds out the prospect of significant increases in pay for productive and competent staff in local authorities, teaching, health, fire, ambulance, regulatory and other services. The salary increases which cannot be afforded in monolithic, nationally bargained public services become possible and indeed necessary in a system based on precise service specification, and competitive tender.

Remedies and Public Provision

An open society must be an honest society. Information must be available to citizens in a manner which permits and encourages sensible decision-making and choice. The first obstacle to the open society is the opaque financing of public provision, which has come to conceal more than it reveals.

It is small wonder that health and welfare provision is bedevilled by insoluble debates on financial under-provision when so much of it is concealed under misleading labels in general taxation. The case for an identified health tax is that it would help to break free from the cynical concept of rationed health care which has persisted under both parties since the War. State pensions can be sustained only by the 'pay-as-you-go' system, which relies upon the preparedness of one generation to pay up for the promises voted to themselves by their parents, without forward funding or insurance worthy of the name.

It is also small wonder that local government finance is subject to continual, repeated review, when so much of the system rests upon central taxpayers subsidising local spending decisions, kept in check only by the crudest of central cash controls. Residents of one local area must see their contributions head off on round trips across the country, to pay for the spending desires of other local communities which have no moral claim on their taxes.

The more serious consequence of these shortcomings is in persistent failure to meet any guaranteed service standards. So if the first limb of empowerment must be a shift to transparent and visible taxes or charges, the second must be enforceable service standards guaranteed by contract from state agencies to citizens.

The problem was illustrated most acutely, and sadly, when the parents of a child in one of the Birmingham heart operation cases sought to go to law to enforce a right for their child to be treated, through the provision of adequate nursing staff. They were told that the NHS provides no such rights; they were left at the mercy of administrative discretion, subject to no enforceable performance standards.

Too much of Britain's public provision still rests on monopoly providers financed by the coercive taxation power of the state, and yielding to no enforceable contract with citizens and customers.

It is a flaw in the modern legislative environment that the system, unless modified to include effective assessments of compliance and other costs, assumes that legislation, and regulation by or under primary or delegated legislation, is likely to be benevolent, disinterested, effective and 'free'. It is assumed to be a good, limited only by the regrettable lack of parliamentary time which inhibits its production.

The powerful thrust to legislate has been most apparent in the United States where, increasingly, attention has turned to the development of additional constitutional constraints on federal government growth. 'Sunset' legislation; Californian propositions; presidential directives requiring competitive tendering; and, most recently and dramatically, the Gramm-Rudman-Hollings deficit reduction legislation are evidence of a continuing attempt to 'box government in' by constraining the ability of legislators to put short-term or vested interests ahead of longer-term objectives. In Britain, although lacking the formal constitutional status, the Medium-Term Financial Strategy represents a broadly similar approach in that it seeks to discipline government behaviour over a period of years. In this case it is the loss of credibility which would result from a dramatic move away from the strategy which is the chief sanction.

It is possible to introduce constraints and checking mechanisms at micro-level, as well. *Torts* may be created by statute as an alternative to regulations enforceable by central authorities, leaving to the market the enforcement and protection of the rights conferred.

Cutting through the regulatory superstructure of the Financial Services Act, the establishment of torts which allow individuals to recover damages directly from wrongdoers could complement compensation funds established by self-regulatory organisations.

Civil penalties provide a cheap and effective means of ensuring that regulatory agencies are under direct economic pressure to fulfil their statutory functions. Granting to individuals the power to recover, in a County Court, a pre-established financial penalty for breach of statutory duty can prove highly effective as a means of keeping the attention of those responsible for the function upon their duties.

The penalty can be adjusted to circumstances. Under the *Public Health Act 1936*, for example, local authorities were made liable to a penalty of 25p per day that refuse was uncollected from household premises, the penalty being recoverable by householders in the County Court. Where any significant number of residents were deprived of refuse collection both publicity and the risk of a large number of compensatory payments encouraged authorities to provide an alternative.

The technique is now beginning to reappear. As a result of an initiative by the Office of Telecommunications, British Telecom has agreed to pay penalty payments of £5 a day to customers whose telephone service is unavailable for more than 48 hours because of its failure to supply or maintain telephone service. Mercury has announced a similar approach.

In the privatisation of electricity supply, distribution companies have been required to credit customer accounts when service is interrupted. There is a wide range of other public services, provided as a monopoly or relying upon public finance, where customer rights are either truncated or excluded. There is scope, again using the contract approach, to ensure that those who suffer economic loss are able to obtain a remedy.

Civil actions for damages can be used in cases of government failure. Actions for negligence against government departments are now common and can include action in respect of ministerial statements, as shown in the 'Chickengate' affair.

This approach is not new, and can be encouraged by building strict liability on government agencies into legislation. An example is the *Riot Damages Act 1889*, by which the obligation of police authorities to secure the effective policing of their areas is re-inforced by the establishment of a right of action in damages for those whose property is damaged as a result of a riot—it being the duty of the authority to prevent riots from damaging property. In a number of cases, public officials have argued that it is administratively inconvenient or otherwise undesirable to enforce the law: providing a direct remedy where they fail to do so redresses the balance.

Specific Techniques

There is scope to extend these techniques. Some particular suggestions are:

o It should be the price of a protected public sector or monopoly position that customers have additional rights to protect them from unsatisfactory service provision unless and until full competition prevails.

o Rail customers, for example, should have enforceable entitlements to refunds and compensation for loss suffered as a result of breach of agreed or reasonable conditions of carriage.

o Local authority housing tenants should be entitled to compensation payments for delay in effecting repairs or failures to maintain housing estates to acceptable standards.

o Telephone, gas and electricity customers should be given clear and explicit entitlements to reductions in bills or repayments for failure to instal appliances, maintain them or meet service appointments.

o NHS patients should be assured of treatment within a limited waiting time beyond which they become empowered to find treatment elsewhere, including in the private sector, at the cost of the NHS service provider.

o The administration of compensation schemes should be removed from the hands of the service provider, where there can be a clear conflict of interest, and handed to consumer councils or regulatory bodies. Service providers would deposit cash bonds to allow them to determine and finance customer compensation directly and without delay.

Decision-making Procedures

The analysis above differs significantly from the analysis made by many other advocates of free markets. The key difference is an emphasis on the central importance of decision-making procedures and the conditions under which decisions are made rather than private ownership or competition. Private ownership and a framework for competition are the institutional conditions for the successful production of market information, but ownership and competition do not furnish an explanation of why it is that the private sector is so much more successful at delivering the goods than the public sector.

Simple dichotomies between state and market, public and private,

85

are not very helpful. Those who continue to emphasise the rôle of the state do not seriously propose to abolish capitalism—that is, a system based upon the relatively free exchange of private property rights between legally autonomous groups and individuals. What they do propose is to administer capitalism on social democratic lines—or what should be more properly called welfare capitalism—a system in which welfare, health and educational services are, at the very least, and in the main guaranteed, secured and paid for by the state.

By focussing on decision-making procedures one can avoid dichotomies and appreciate the extent to which decision-making procedures are subject to market incentives or administrative discretion. Administrative and political discretion is of course a major component of decision-making procedures in private sector organisations as well as in public sector ones. However, administrative discretion in the private sector is tempered and largely determined by the economic incentives which the decision-makers face.

The most successful corporations have for a long time recognised the importance of providing decision-makers with the right incentives and information. This is why many companies have increased individual contracts of employment, created competition between divisions, set up individual cost and profit centres, spread performance-related pay, and made the budgets of individual operations partly dependent upon their performance. All these reforms improve the discovery procedures at work within companies because they create incentives for employees to be entrepreneurs within their own company, and to act upon the information which is at their disposal.

Reducing Administrative and Regulatory Discretion
The main aim of public sector reforms should be to diminish administrative discretion wherever possible. Administrative discretion should give way to decision-making according to market information, financial incentives and clearly defined general rules.

By the year 2000, one can expect virtually every major public utility and nationalised industry to be in private hands, including rail and coal. One can also expect, with an extension of compulsory competitive tendering, that many more council services will be delivered by private contractors, though service specification and regulation will be left in the hands of council officers.[10]

---

[10] I have assessed some of these changes in a chapter in John Stewart and Gerry Stoker (eds.), *What Future for Local Government?*, London: Macmillan, 1989.

Many council officers and departments of state will see a marked shift in their rôle. They will be responsible for securing, guaranteeing and regulating service delivery, but they will no longer be involved in the actual delivery of particular services. Rates of pay and organisational structure and methods of service delivery will cease to be the business of civil servants and council officers. Instead they will face the challenge of regulating government-created markets in such a way that the enormous benefits of competition can be harnessed while at the same time ensuring that private shareholders do not gain at the expense of the public.

Regulation will remain an important aspect of public sector reforms. However, the drawing of the line between the state and the market, which will become even hazier than it is now, should not be fixed in advance by regulators. Instead the market should effectively determine the line between state and market, or rather the degree of regulation.

Regulators should respond to developments in the market and devise or administer regulations in a way that recognises market trends and allows for as much market development as is feasible. Regulators should respond to market signals and have as little room as possible for administrative discretion. Any non-market criteria they use for the regulation of markets should be based on very clear guidelines and general principles, and it should be possible for a private supplier to ask for compensation and to challenge in an independent court any ruling by a regulator which is against his interests.

Contract Model

The administrative model of service delivery and control in the public sector should give way to the contract model. This model gives maximum scope for the introduction of the market or else relies upon the maximum possible use of mechanisms which mimic the market, although the presumption should always be in favour of actual markets wherever possible. The term 'contract model' emphasises that the relationship between the service deliverer and the service recipient should be seen as an implicit contract. The contract model should become the model for re-organisation in those areas of the public and quasi-public sector which for historical and structural reasons cannot be opened up entirely to the free play of market forces. Those responsible for providing the services in these sectors should be governed by a legally enforceable contract which specifies the standards to which those services should be provided. Failure to do so should generate penalties payable to those damaged to redress their loss.

These definitions are best contained in explicit 'contracts', which are fixed term, open to competitive tender, and supervised by the National Audit Office. In place, they can strengthen the separate interests of specifiers and providers of services, tightening accountability, democratic control and cost effectiveness.

When approached in this way, the core rôles necessarily fulfilled by direct employees of government are extremely limited. Once public sector managers see the opportunities of greater independence, less politicisation, new financial rewards comparable with those in the private sector, opportunities for management buy-outs, equity investment and all the challenges of a career which combines business efficiency with public service there is likely to be a powerful demand from managers to adopt the new structures.

This model of the contract state is important if one is serious about empowerment—increasing the freedom that citizens have to control their own lives. Increasing prosperity and the flourishing of competition in the private sector has meant that citizens have experienced vastly increased control over their own affairs at home, at work and in the commercial market-place. However, citizens have very little control over their affairs when they have to rely on the state sector. Power, in the form of administrative discretion, must be wrested from the producers and countervailing powers placed in the hands of consumers.

More broadly, the view of government as a series of contracts makes it easier to secure this integration.

o It separates the political process of determination of objectives and specification of services from their delivery, removing conflict of interest which occurs when those specifying a service are also its deliverers.

o It reduces the public choice phenomenon of lobbying for bureaucratic expansion by introducing built-in competitive pressures.

o It facilitates regular review of policy objectives by requiring regular re-assessment and re-specification within a democratic framework.

o It strengthens opportunities for quality control and concentration of resources on supervision and compliance.

○ It regularises relationships between central government and local authorities and competing agencies.

○ It is a force for transparency of funding.

○ It is compatible with earmarking of finance to measurable service delivery, developing the model of the community charge.

○ It is compatible with specific remedies and new enforcement powers for individuals who have suffered loss by reason of government failure, or the failure of agencies granted monopoly or other enhanced powers by the state.

For too long government has treated citizens as mere recipients or clients of the public sector and a passive recipient of poor quality services. It has seen government as authority, as power, as a high authority over individual lives. Successive models of the state have welshed on their side of the social contract. It is time to give the citizen the powers to be a consumer in the public sector, and make sure that government is on tap, not on top.

APPENDIX 1

Executive Agencies Established as at 1 October 1991

Executive Agency	Date of establishment	Staff numbers
Accounts Service Agency	1.10.91	90
Building Research Establishment	2. 4.90	690
CADW (Welsh Historic Monuments)	2. 4.91	220
Central Office of Information[1]	5. 4.90	680
Central Veterinary Laboratory	2. 4.90	600
Chemical and Biological Defence Establishment[2]	2. 4.91	600
Civil Service College	6. 6.89	230
Companies House	3.10.88	1,100
Defence Research Agency	2. 4.91	12,300
Directorate General of Defence Accounts[2]	1. 4.91	2,150
Driver and Vehicle Licensing Agency	2. 4.90	5,250
Driving Standards Agency	2. 4.90	2,100
Employment Service	2. 4.90	34,500
Forensic Science Service	1. 4.91	600
Historic Royal Palaces	1.10.89	340
Historic Scotland	2. 4.91	610
HMSO[1]	14.12.88	3,250
Hydrographic Office[2]	6. 4.90	870
Insolvency Service	21. 3.90	1,500
Intervention Board	2. 4.90	940
Laboratory of the Government Chemist	3.10.89	340
Land Registry	2. 7.90	10,050
Medicines Control Agency	11. 7.91	310
Meteorological Office	2. 4.90	2,300
Military Survey[2]	2. 4.91	1,230
National Engineering Laboratory	5.10.90	380
National Physical Laboratory	3. 7.90	830
National Weights & Measures Laboratory	18. 4.89	50
Natural Resources Unit	2. 4.90	420
NHS Estates	1. 4.91	120
Occupational Health Service	2. 4.90	100
Ordnance Survey	1. 5.90	2,450
Patent Office	1. 3.90	1,200
QEII Conference Centre	6. 7.89	70

Executive Agency	Date of establishment	Staff numbers
Radiocommunications Agency	2. 4.90	500
RAF Maintenance[2]	2. 4.91	13,000
Rate Collection Agency (Northern Ireland)	2. 4.91	270
Recruitment and Assessment Services Agency	2. 4.91	260
Registers of Scotland	6. 4.90	1,200
Royal Mint[1]	2. 4.90	1,050
Scottish Fisheries Protection Agency	12. 4.91	200
Service Children's Schools (North West Europe)[2]	24. 4.91	2,330
Social Security Agency (Northern Ireland Civil Service)	1. 7.91	5,500
Social Security Benefits Agency	2. 4.91	65,500
Social Security Contributions Agency	2. 4.91	7,200
Social Security Information Technology Services Agency	2. 4.90	3,600
Social Security Resettlement Agency	24. 5.89	470
Training and Employment Agency (Northern Ireland)	2. 4.90	1,700
UK Passport Agency	2. 4.91	1,200
Valuation Office	30. 9.91	5,250
Vehicle Certification Agency	2. 4.90	80
Vehicle Inspectorate[1]	1. 8.88	1,850
Veterinary Medicines Directorate	2. 4.90	80
Warren Spring Laboratory	20. 4.89	310
Wilton Park Conference Centre	1. 9.91	30
No. of Agencies = 55		200,150
Customs & Excise[3]		27,000
Total No. of Staff:[4]		**227,150**
Total No. of Civil Servants:		**217,790**

[1] Trading Funds.   [2] Defence Support Agency.

[3] Moving towards full operation on Next Steps lines following publication of Framework Documents.

[4] Includes 8,060 Armed Forces personnel in MOD Agencies, and 1,300 locally engaged staff in Service Children's Schools (North West Europe).

Figures exclude casuals and are full-time Civil Servants employed on 1 April 1991 (part-time staff counted as half units).

APPENDIX 2

Next Steps—Activities Announced by Departments as Under Consideration for Agency Status as at 1 October 1991

	Staff Nos. *(at 1 April 1991)*
ADAS Agency	2,500
Agricultural Scientific Services	140
Central Science Laboratory	350
Central Statistical Office	1,050
Chessington Computer Centre	450
Child Support Agency (Northern Ireland)[1]	not yet known
Common Services Division[2]	1,730
Criminal Compensation (Northern Ireland)	140
Defence Animal Centre[2]	140
Defence Operational Analysis Establishment[2]	180
Defence Statistics Organisation[2]	170
Directorate Information Technology Bureau Services[2]	120
Driver and Vehicle Testing Agency (Northern Ireland)	250
Drivers Vehicles and Operators Information Technology[3]	
Duke of York's Royal Military School	100
Fire Service College	190
Fuel Suppliers Branch	20
MOD Police[2]	4,260
Naval Aircraft Repair Organisation[2]	1,470
Ordnance Survey (Northern Ireland)	200
Pesticide Safety Division	160
Planning Inspectorate	630
Property Holdings Portfolio Management	420
Public Record Office	440
Queen Victoria School	60
RAF Training[2]	11,450
Royal Parks	580
Scottish Prisons	4,000
Social Security Child Support Agency[4]	not yet known

	Staff Nos. (at 1 April 1991)
Teachers' Pensions Branch	290
The Buying Agency[5]	80
Transport Road Research Laboratory	580
Youth Treatment Service	210
No. of Activities = 33	32,360
Inland Revenue[6] (excl. Valuation Office)	60,450
Total No. of Staff: [7]	**92,810**
Total No. of Civil Servants:	**84,240**

[1] Estimated to require 700 staff, of which 120 will come from the Social Security Agency (Northern Ireland).

[2] Defence Support Agency.

[3] Currently part of DVLA staffed by 500.

[4] From early 1993 the Agency is estimated to require 4,500 staff, 1,500 of which will come from the Social Security Benefits Agency.

[5] Trading Fund.

[6] Moving towards full operation on Next Steps lines in accordance with the Action Plan of February 1991: 34 Executive Offices by April 1992, each with a Framework Document, sharper accountabilities and wider managerial freedoms.

[7] Includes 8,570 Armed Forces personnel in Defence Support Agency candidates.

Figures exclude casuals and are full-time Civil Servants employed on 1 April 1991 (part-time staff counted as half units).

6

THE CABINET
AND 'NEXT STEPS'

Lord Hunt of Tanworth, GCB
Formerly Secretary of the Cabinet, 1973-79

AFTER THE PRESENT Prime Minister took office there was much talk about a return to collective Cabinet government. No doubt this was largely a question of style. Prime Ministers (like anyone else) use different tactics to achieve their ends, and there have always been some who lead from the front and others who prefer to have the last word in a discussion: and indeed, recent events showed that no Prime Minister can survive without the support of the Cabinet. *Plus ça change . . .* Nevertheless, this is perhaps an opportune time to reflect on one aspect of the Cabinet's collective rôle which is new.

The origin of Cabinet government and collective responsibility is well known. Unlike most countries Britain has no chief executive. As the Crown retreated to become a constitutional symbol rather than the unifying and motive force of the executive, so Parliament vested all executive power in departmental Ministers. Formally, the Prime Minister barely exists in our constitution and has no formal authority simply to override his colleagues in the way that an American President treats cabinet officers as no more than advisers. A collective executive, or collective responsibility, emerged as the means, under the Prime Minister's chairmanship, of providing stable and co-ordinated government. Thus Ministers have a clear responsibility for the decisions of their colleagues as well as for their own.

Evolution of Cabinet Committees

This worked well enough when the issues of the day were self-contained and largely untechnical and when Ministers had plenty of time on their hands. The enlarged and more complicated rôle of the modern state made life increasingly difficult for them, particularly in the discharge of their collective responsibility for the problems of their colleagues. Thus devices like Cabinet Committees were introduced to buttress the system. It is a system which can lead to delay and compromise but most people still agree that a collective executive as a means of providing unity to the British system of government is worth its rather cumbrous nature for the advantages of shared discussion and decision. As Churchill once put it, 'it is the worst of all possible forms of government, except for all the others'.

This is not the place to discuss whether modern pressures—including the demands of the media, the need to articulate policy at the European Council and other summits, and the way in which Prime Minister's Questions have evolved in the House of Commons—are pushing the Prime Minister into filling what was always something of a hole at the centre of our decision-taking process. It is, however, arguable that recent organisational changes within government will call for a new kind of rôle for Ministers collectively.

It is perhaps a truism to say that Cabinets are best at taking one-off decisions with a high political content and least good at monitoring the results of their decisions *ex post facto*. A new kind of monitoring is, however, going to be needed as Ministers devolve more and more of the work for which they have hitherto been directly accountable to other bodies with whom they will have an arm's-length relationship.

'Next Steps': The Role of Executive Agencies

Already over 50 Executive Agencies have been established with more to come. Some of them are very large, for example the Benefits Agency, the Contributions Agency, the Employment Service Agency, the Passports Agency, and so on. Indeed the 'Next Steps' initiative will have been applied to more than half the civil service. Nor is this the end of the story. In an interesting report published in May 1991, the Prime Minister's Adviser on Efficiency said:

> '[T]here are already signs of their [the Next Steps principles] spreading across from the executive parts of government to influence the way central government as a whole conducts its business, with a growing pattern of

personal responsibility for discrete and substantial blocks of work, devolved budgeting and explicit agreement over performance targets.'[1]

There is also more talk of increased 'contractorisation', or competitive tendering, for public services. Finally, the Citizen's Charter is relevant insofar as it applies to the executive functions of central government, although it is more concerned with the standards of service which the public can expect than with the relationship between Executive Agencies and Ministers.

Few people would dissent from the underlying principles of Next Steps aimed at greater efficiency and cost-effectiveness. Ministers set clear output targets; and Chief Executives of Agencies are accountable for meeting them and are judged accordingly. This new kind of relationship will, however, have to avoid two opposite extremes.

The first is Ministerial or Departmental neo-colonialism. This would take the form of over-zealous monitoring or second-guessing, thus failing to give agencies their head and demotivating their personnel. Private sector companies which have successfully divisionalised or moved to a holding company structure have quickly realised that this is not the same as delegation. The centre needs certain very specific controls but they are a quite different kind of control to what was needed before and where they do not apply the business unit must be free to get on with the job unimpeded.

The opposite extreme would be to rely solely on financial targets. This is the approach which, for example, the Hanson Group adopts. You give your subsidiaries specific guidelines in relation to investment, cash flow and profit, and these are monitored closely. But otherwise the subsidiaries run themselves and devise their own strategy. This kind of control, although perhaps meeting the needs of the Treasury, would not be acceptable in the case of agencies providing a monopoly service to the general public and where Ministers will have legitimate interest in the quality of the service provided. Financial performance, important though it is, cannot be the only criterion.

Ministerial Control

The problem will therefore be to devise a system of well-informed Ministerial control which falls well clear of bureaucratic intrusion. This will inevitably involve judgement as well as measurement for the

---

[1] Foreword to *Making the Most of Next Steps: the Management of Ministers' Departments and their Agencies*, London: HMSO, May 1991.

reason given in the previous paragraph. Much can be done through the Framework Document when the agency is established. This should clearly define its aims, the resources available to it, the freedom (and limits) for the Chief Executive, the targets, and how politically sensitive matters are to be handled. It is the key to the Next Steps concept, but it will be difficult to couch it in specific rather than general terms, and Departments will be feeling their way. When it comes to targets and performance indicators, the problem of balancing measurement and judgement will be even more difficult. It was put well in an interesting report prepared for the Polytechnics and Colleges Funding Council which quotes Professor John Sizer (Professor of Financial Management at Loughborough University of Technology):

> 'Peer review and performance indicators should and must complement each other. In the absence of performance indicators, the element of judgement may be too great: reliance on performance indicators in the absence of peer judgements is extremely dangerous.'[2]

The report of the Prime Minister's Efficiency Unit mentioned above sees the devising of targets and performance indicators as solely a matter for individual sponsoring departments once the initial framework has been established, and that at this stage 'the central departments should be able to withdraw from the detail of management of executive operations'. This must be right to the extent that another level of central monitoring—still less back-seat driving or second-guessing—must be avoided. On the other hand, the report appears also to be lukewarm about the case for the centre taking a responsibility for 'suggesting and supporting solutions which would assist agencies to manage their business better as opposed to challenging and seeking flaws'. This may be pushing disengagement too far, and there are two reasons why Ministers collectively should concern themselves about it.

Code of Practice for Agencies

The first is that a very large and important part of the civil service is now navigating in unknown waters and with few navigational aids. The old order has gone: but if, where services to the public are concerned, financial performance indicators have to be supplemented both by other output figures and by an element of judgement, then private

---

[2] *Performance Indicators*, Report of the Committee of Enquiry (Chairman: Alfred Morris), Bristol: Polytechnics and Colleges Funding Council, June 1990, p. 7.

sector experience of monitoring profit centres will not always provide a convenient rule of thumb. The staff of the new agencies will also lack experience of an arm's-length relationship with their sponsors which is quite different from previous Ministerial sponsorship. There will therefore be a real need for cross-fertilisation of experience and techniques so that while accepting, to take a far-fetched example, that the output of the Meteorological Office cannot be measured in exactly the same way as the output of the Insolvency Service (both of them Next Steps agencies), nevertheless something like a code of best agency/departmental practice might evolve.

The second reason for collective Ministerial interest is that while Ministers are rightly relinquishing day-to-day control over the executive activities of government, many of the agencies will remain very big spenders indeed. Bids for resources in the annual public expenditure exercise will increasingly be justified by performance indicators. 'It's worthwhile putting money into X because it is beating its output target.' No doubt, but what does this in practice mean? How robust was the target, how significant its achievement? The setting of targets in areas where financial performance is not the sole criterion will be difficult enough from the technical point of view but it will be essential to have clear targets which cannot be fudged to suit the outcome.

'A New Kind of Guidance and Monitoring'

None of this implies a criticism of progress made by Next Steps to date. On the contrary. The Cabinet are, however, overseeing a very large and significant reform and, like the boards of successful decentralised private sector companies, they should recognise that decentralisation also requires a new and different kind of central guidance and monitoring. The value of Framework Documents, however good the concept, will depend on the way they are used. Whatever the agreement says, a Department may interfere too much or alternatively take an excessively *laissez-faire* attitude. Another danger is that a department and an agency may have too cosy a relationship so that targets are insufficiently demanding or performance comparisons are fudged. There will be a need for something akin to a code of best practice both in terms of performance measurement and also in ensuring that, while agencies are given their freedom as far as possible, certain principles of fairness and public service continue to be observed in the interests of collective Cabinet government.

The Cabinet, as a collective entity, should have an interest in ensuring that the relationship between departments and agencies is monitored and that lessons are learned. The task could be given to the Efficiency Unit. A better solution might be to establish an Inspector General of Executive Agencies who, in consultation with the Head of the Civil Service and the Treasury, could periodically review the performance of each department/agency combination and report to the Prime Minister on how the agencies are managing to combine the drive for greater managerial independence and efficiency with service principally to their customers but also to collective Cabinet government. The prime objective would be to encourage the development of the system rather than to harass individual cases and to ensure cross-learning and good practice. Otherwise there may be a risk of greater differences—of ethics as well as performance—than Ministers would wish.

7

LOCAL GOVERNMENT TAXATION: THE LOGIC OF A LOCAL INCOME TAX*

David N. King
University of Stirling

Twenty Years of Concern With Local Government Finance

LOCAL GOVERNMENT TAXATION has been a 'topical' issue in the United Kingdom for many years. There have been no less than four Green Papers addressing the question in the last two decades (HMSO, 1971, 1977, 1981 and 1986). The first three of these all advocated the retention of a property tax, at least for the foreseeable future, but each also mooted significant reforms: the 1971 paper envisaged the possibility of extra local taxes; the 1977 paper envisaged reforming rates, chiefly by moving over to capital valuations; and the 1981 paper envisaged both extra local taxes and reforms to rates. However, only the 1986 paper actually resulted in any significant changes to local taxation. But these changes, most notably the replacement of the property tax on homes by a poll tax, have proved so unpopular that a 'Yellow' Paper has now appeared (DoE, 1991) advocating a banded property tax—or council tax—as a replacement for the poll tax from 1993. Moreover, the Government has increased the level of grants to local authorities so that the poll

---

*This chapter is a revised version of 'Local Government Taxation: The Way Ahead', first published as *IEA Inquiry* No. 24 in March 1991.

tax and future council tax will finance only about 15 per cent of local spending.

It is worth mentioning this background because it forces us to consider why governments have been struggling so unsuccessfully with the issue for two decades. If we can identify an underlying difficulty, then perhaps that will help us to identify a satisfactory solution.

It might seem that the underlying difficulty is simply that there is no ideal local tax, with the result that any system that is in place will always seem ripe for change. If this were the underlying difficulty, then we ought to find that major local tax reform is also permanently on the agenda in other countries. But while reforms do occur abroad, these are typically modest; and few countries seem to have found the issue as intractable as it has been found here. Indeed, the experience of other OECD countries shows a remarkable consensus on the choice of state or local taxes, as shown in columns (1)-(4) of Table 1 which covers all OECD countries except Luxembourg (for which insufficient data are available). In 1988, income taxes were by far the most popular subcentral taxes: income taxes were the principal source of subcentral tax revenue in 14 of the 22 countries. A local property tax was the principal subcentral tax in only five countries. No other subcentral tax was nearly as popular as these two.

The Localist and Centralist Approaches

A more plausible underlying difficulty is that successive United Kingdom governments seem not to have decided what local government is for. Interestingly, this question lay at the centre of the discussions of the Layfield Committee of Inquiry into Local Government Finance (HMSO, 1976). There are essentially two alternative approaches that a central government can adopt towards local authorities. On one approach, local authorities can be seen as independent, democratically elected bodies intended to provide certain services in quantities and qualities desired by local citizens, though there may be the occasional constraint applied from the centre, for instance to control the authorities when their actions impinge on non-residents. On the other approach, local authorities can be seen as effectively agents of the central government, implementing national policies with the occasional discretion here and there. The Layfield Committee referred to these options as the localist and the centralist approaches.

It is critically important for the central government to decide which approach to adopt, for, as the Layfield Committee noted, the two

TABLE 1

OECD COUNTRIES 1988: (A) STATE AND LOCAL TAX YIELDS AS A PERCENTAGE OF GDP; AND (B) GNP PER HEAD

| Country | (A) State and local tax yields as a percentage of GDP: | | | | | | (B) GNP per head ($) | Rank |
	Income (1)	Property (2)	Sales (3)	Other (4)	Total (5)	Rank (6)	(7)	(8)
1 Denmark	14·4	1·2	–	–	15·6	1	18,450	8
2 Sweden	15·2	–	0·1	–	15·3	2	19,300	5
3 Canada	5·7	3·2	4·6	1·6	15·1	3	16,960	9
4 Switzerland	9·8	1·9	0·1	0·4	12·2	4	27,500	1
5 Germany	7·8	1·1	2·2	0·4	11·5	5	18,480	7
6 Finland	9·6	0·1	–	–	9·7	6	18,590	6
7 Norway	8·7	0·7	–	0·3	9·7	7	19,990	3
8 United States	2·4	2·9	3·3	0·7	9·3	8	19,840	4
9 Austria	3·9	0·5	3·4	1·2	9·0	9	15,470	11
10 Japan	4·9	1·8	0·9	0·4	8·0	10	21,020	2
11 Australia	–	2·8	0·7	2·6	6·1	11	12,340	16
12 France	0·6	1·3	0·2	1·8	3·9	12	16,090	10
13 United Kingdom	–	3·9	–	–	3·9	13	12,810	15
14 Spain	1·2	1·0	1·1	0·4	3·7	14	7,740	19
15 Belgium	1·7	–	–	0·6	2·3	15	14,490	13
16 Turkey	1·0	0·1	0·8	0·4	2·3	16	1,280	22
17 New Zealand	–	1·9	–	0·1	2·0	17	10,000	17
18 Portugal	0·8	0·4	0·6	0·1	1·9	18	3,650	21
19 Netherlands	–	0·8	–	0·3	1·1	19	14,520	12
20 Ireland	–	0·9	–	–	0·9	20	7,750	18
21 Italy	0·3	–	0·1	0·2	0·6	21	13,330	14
22 Greece	–	–	0·1	0·3	0·4	22	4,800	20
Unweighted average	4·0	1·2	0·8	0·5	6·6	–	14,290	–

Sources: Revenue Statistics of OECD Member Countries 1965-69, Paris: OECD, 1970, pp. 177 and 179; *World Development Report 1990*, Oxford: Oxford University Press for the World Bank, 1991, pp. 178-79.

approaches lead to quite different prescriptions about local finance. The localist approach requires that most local spending should be financed by local taxes while the centralist approach requires that most local spending should be financed by grants from the central government. The Layfield Committee defended these conclusions by saying that

'whoever is responsible for spending money should also be responsible for raising it so that the amount of expenditure is subject to democratic control' (HMSO, 1976, p. 283).

But it is worth looking at the arguments a little more fully.

On the localist approach, a high degree of local tax revenue is required for at least three reasons. First, local politicians, bureaucrats and voters may be more prudent in their decisions if they are spending money raised locally than if they are spending money that has been given to them.

Secondly, local taxes are necessary to enable local authorities to vary the quantities and qualities of their services in accordance with local wishes. It may be argued that local authorities can alter their service provision even if they have taxes that account for only a modest share of their spending. For instance, they can currently vary the community charge which now accounts for 15 per cent of local income. But relying on taxes which raise only a small fraction of income is not satisfactory. Suppose that today an authority wishes to raise its income by, say, 7·5 per cent. Then it must raise its community charge by 50 per cent. Such a rise gives misleading signals to local voters, and it may well be opposed on the grounds that it takes the community charge far above 'reasonable' levels.

Thirdly, and perhaps most importantly, when a government pays grants, it is likely to want to control how local authorities spend them. Indeed, arguably it *should* control how grant receipts are spent as it is accountable to its national taxpayers for this money. Admittedly, central governments do not always constrain the spending of those to whom they pay money. For example, the recipients of transfer payments—such as unemployment benefit, state pensions and child benefit—are allowed to spend the receipts as they choose. But this is probably because it would be politically unacceptable and practically difficult to introduce constraints on how individual citizens spend money given to them by the government. There seem to be no such difficulties protecting institutions such as local authorities from controls on how they may spend any money which the government gives to them.

On the localist approach, then, local authorities should be able to raise most of their money from local taxes. In contrast, if the government takes the centralist view and regards local authorities as existing to provide centrally ordained services, then it should provide them with grants to cover most of their costs. This is chiefly because it is inappropriate for the government to be able to insist that services are provided if it does not have to raise the money needed; the government is far more likely to take a responsible view about how much local expenditure to require if it has to raise the money itself. Also, it seems inappropriate for the central government to compel local authorities to raise local taxes from local voters if there is negligible local discretion over how that money may be spent. Of course, on the centralist approach there is a case for allowing local authorities to have just one small tax to finance marginal changes to spending levels.

A Middle Way?

Unfortunately, past Green Papers—and the recent Yellow Paper—have avoided choosing between the centralist and localist approaches. The issue was considered only in the 1977 paper which was prepared in the wake of the Layfield Committee's report, and this paper rejected both approaches. Instead it advocated a 'middle way'. On this basis, local spending was to continue being financed with local taxes and grants, each contributing roughly equal shares.

The middle way may sound attractive in principle, but it is surely unworkable in practice. The point is that so long as we have local elections it is important for local voters and local politicians to know precisely what discretion local authorities have. This is easy on the localist approach—they have discretion except where stated otherwise. It is also easy on the centralist approach—they have no discretion except where stated otherwise. If governments really want to operate a middle way, then they should cover every single possible local activity and say whether local discretion was permitted and, if it was, how much freedom was permitted. This would be very difficult to do and it would be very bewildering to voters.

In practice, of course, governments in this country have loosely pursued a middle way, but they have not defined it at all clearly. This muddled approach lies at the root of much of the conflict between central government and local government. Two classic examples are

105

the controversies which surrounded the imposition of comprehensive schools and the forcible selling of council homes. Some local authorities claimed their voters had given them a mandate to retain selective schools and some claimed their voters had given them a mandate not to sell council homes. Yet the relevant central governments claimed their voters had given them mandates to force local authorities to have comprehensive schools and to force them to sell council homes. A situation where two levels of government can each claim opposing mandates on the same issue is a recipe for conflict and makes a mockery of democracy. It is far better to try to draw up clear demarcation lines for local authority discretion.

The present confusion and conflict between central and local government is aggravated by the mixed system of finance. Local authorities claim that they should be able to spend local taxes as they please while central governments undoubtedly feel that their payments of grants give them the right to interfere. In principle, there would be less of a problem if it was clear which items of local spending were covered by local taxes and which by central grants, but of course both sources of finance are simply paid into the same accounts.

The Localist Approach and Economic Control

Historically, elected local authorities were established on the localist approach. The earliest elected authorities were the 13th-century boroughs which were set up, partly at least, to allow their citizens freedom from the shire reeves. The shire reeves were central government officials who retained power elsewhere in their respective shires. So the origin of local government constitutes one argument for the localist approach. Another, more important, argument stems from considering that public expenditure accounts for over 40 per cent of gross national product (GNP). With so much money being spent by the government sector as a whole, there is much to be said for the localist solution and, wherever feasible, allowing local authorities to cater for varying tastes. If some government sector activity is inevitable, then it seems much more satisfactory to allow the package of policies to vary from area to area than to have the central government impose a uniform package of policies on everyone.

While none of the past Green Papers has advocated the localist approach, they have been inclined to nod favourably in the direction of local autonomy, only to follow this up by saying that the central government must control local authorities because local spending seriously affects the economy. For instance, the 1971 Green Paper said that

'the government wish to give greater freedom to local authorities, but they cannot evade their own responsibility for management of the national economy' (p. 6).

The alleged need to control local authorities for macro-economic purposes leads naturally to arguing for limited local tax power.

However, there is no theoretical reason to suppose that local spending does seriously affect the national economy. For instance, when authorities decide to spend more, they have to raise local taxes, so private spending falls and there is a negligible net rise in aggregate demand. If local authorities decided to spend 10 per cent more in 1991, this would of itself add about £4 billion to aggregate demand. But local authorities would have to raise £4 billion more from poll tax payers. Of this, about a sixth would come from extra poll tax rebates, so that poll tax payers would actually be worse off by some £3·3 billion. As a result, they might cut their consumption spending by around £3 billion. So the net effect on aggregate demand would be a rise of £1 billion, that is, £4 billion more local spending minus £3 billion less consumer spending. This net rise of £1 billion is very small compared to total demand which is about £600 billion, so the substantial rise in local spending would have little effect. Moreover, if the government were worried by it, then it could cut grants to local authorities and force local taxes up more. Or at least it could usually do so, though it may be reluctant to do so if local authorities have as their only tax one that is very unpopular.

Practice confirms this theoretical proposition that local tax power does not disturb economic management. If it did, then countries with high degrees of state or local tax power should fare badly. But it is clear from columns (6) and (8) of Table 1 that they do not. Table 1 shows all the OECD countries (except Luxembourg) ranked according to the extent of total state and local taxes as a percentage of gross domestic product (GDP). The ranks are shown in column (6). Column (8) shows their ranking in terms of GNP per head. In fact, the countries at the top of the table tend to have the most successful economies. Indeed, statistically speaking, there is a highly significant correlation between substantial devolved taxes and high GNP per head. So it really is not acceptable for any government to eschew the localist approach for macro-economic reasons.

Financing the Centralist Approach

The discussion so far argues that the Government will not satisfactorily solve the issue of local government finance unless it makes up its mind whether to adopt a centralist approach or a localist one. The recent fall in local tax levels to around 15 per cent of local spending suggests that, implicitly, the Government may well believe in the centralist approach. But the Government certainly has not stated explicitly that it has adopted this approach, so there must still be some uncertainty about what future rôle it does see for local authorities. If it does eventually opt for the centralist approach, then it may well decide to increase its grants to local authorities even more and leave local authorities with very little in the way of local taxes. They would need only enough tax power to make the very modest changes that they would be allowed to make to their spending levels. Both a small local income tax and a property tax would be reasonably satisfactory—indeed in principle even a very small poll tax could prove sufficient. Probably the property tax would be the best choice here. The reason is that the administration costs are lowest. There is no point in having a tax that is costly to administer if it is intended only to produce a small yield.

Financing the Localist Approach

However, both history and the value of variety point to the localist approach while macro-economics provides no sound argument against it. Suppose the Government did decide to opt for the localist approach. What would this suggest for local taxation? The starting point to answering this question is to remember that the localist approach requires local authorities to finance most of their spending through local taxes. At present, local spending accounts for around 8·5 per cent of GDP. (This spending figure ignores local authority spending on transfers such as housing benefit, student grants and community charge benefits. Local authorities effectively handle these transfers for the central government on an agency basis and they rightly use earmarked grants to finance them.)

Given that local authority spending is some 8·5 per cent of GDP, the localist approach suggests that local taxes should have a yield of at least 6 per cent of GDP, preferably more. How could this be achieved?

It certainly cannot be achieved with a poll tax on its own! Given that the introduction of the poll tax was opposed by all the parties except the Conservatives, and given that the present Conservative

Government has decided to abandon it, it is unlikely that there will ever be a political will to have one again. Even if there were a political will to have a poll tax, the potential yield would be small. The poll tax now has a yield little over 1 per cent of GDP and it must be doubtful whether anything much over 1 per cent would ever be risked in future.

Nor can the target of at least 6 per cent of GDP be achieved with a property tax on its own. Column 2 of Table 1 shows that in OECD countries in 1988, the United Kingdom's property tax accounted for almost 4 per cent of GDP. This tax was by far the highest property tax in the OECD, and it had over three times the (unweighted) average burden of property taxes in the OECD. International experience suggests that around 3 per cent is the upper acceptable limit for a property tax. But remember that this includes the yield on both domestic and non-domestic properties. The ceiling for a local tax on domestic properties alone must be around 1·5 per cent.

How about combining a domestic property tax with a poll tax? Such a combination would obviously be able to raise more income than either on its own; and a poll tax might just be more acceptable if it was combined with another tax. Unfortunately, however, the upper acceptable limit for a property tax and poll tax combination is probably at most 2·5 per cent of GDP—1·5 per cent for the property tax and 1 per cent for the poll tax. Even if a tax on non-domestic property were added in, the feasible yield rises by only 1·5 per cent to 4 per cent which is far too low.

It is clear from an examination of columns (1) to (4) of Table 1 that if local authorities are to raise 6 per cent of GDP in local taxes, then they must have a local income tax. Admittedly, there are sizeable decentralised sales taxes in Canada and the United States, but these are chiefly levied at the province or state level. No country has a sizeable local authority sales tax since there are always worries that local authorities could not raise their tax rates for fear of driving shoppers elsewhere. The Table shows that there are few other local taxes with high yields. The only notable exception is a payroll tax, as used in Australia and Canada, but if there is to be a tax on wages, then for accountability reasons it seems much more sensible to tax employees rather than employers.

This brief analysis suggests that, on the localist approach, a local income tax must be used. The only question is whether to add in another tax as well. There is much to be said for doing so from the government's point of view, because it would ease the burden of income taxation. And there is much to be said for doing so in the interests of sound local taxation. The main reason is that with a local income tax alone, around a quarter of all adults would pay no local tax. This would be unsatisfactory for two reasons. First, there seems to be a moral hazard problem if many voters are entitled to representation without taxation. Secondly, if the majority of voters are paying more than their 'fair' share, then the majority may vote for low levels of local spending, and as a result local services may not be at the levels that electors really want.

Which tax might most appropriately supplement a local income tax to help ensure that everyone paid something? A modest domestic property tax would do, and so would a modest poll tax. In principle, there seem to be two reasons for preferring a poll tax. First, from an administrative point of view the need to decide where everyone lives applies to both an income tax and a poll tax, so there could be economies from some jointness in administration. Secondly, given that the problem with an income tax is that not everyone pays it, there is something to be said for complementing it with a poll tax which everyone does (or at least should) pay. There is also something to be said for combining a local income tax with both a domestic property tax *and* a poll tax, for such a combination would ease the overall income tax burden that people would face. In practice, however, the unpopularity of the poll tax means that any government seeking a supplement for a local income tax would probably opt for a property tax.

Tax Rates on the Localist Approach

It is worth considering what sort of tax rates might emerge if the Government wanted a local income tax combined with a modest property tax—or, perhaps, a local income tax on its own—to raise 6 per cent of GDP. What sort of yield can be squeezed out of a domestic property tax? It was argued above that 1·5 per cent of GDP seems to be about the maximum. However, the Government is committed to introducing its new property tax—or council tax—with a yield comparable to the present yield of the poll tax which is little over 1 per cent, and it is convenient to use this slightly lower and rounder number as the potential yield of a property tax. If such a tax were combined with a local income tax, and if the combined target yield was 6 per cent of GDP, then the local income tax would have to have a yield of 5 per cent of GDP. This would require a local income tax rate of some 17·5p. Of course, every pound that local authorities secured from this new

KING: *Local Government Taxation*

local income tax would reduce by one pound the amount of central government grants that they would require. In turn it would reduce by one pound the amount of income tax revenue that the central government would need. So the average local income tax rate of 17·5p would be matched by a 17·5p drop in central income tax rates from 25p (for the standard rate) to 7·5p. For the typical household, this scenario would simply mean continuing to pay the new council tax and continuing to pay the same amount in income tax, though over two-thirds of its income tax payments would go straight to local authorities.

If the Government decided to have only a local income tax for local authorities, and wanted this to raise the full 6 per cent of GDP, then the rate of local income tax would have to rise from 17·5p to 21p. This rise of 3·5p would not be offset by any fall in central income tax rates, so households would pay more income tax than they do now. But here the compensation would be that the new council tax would be scrapped. So there would be no poll tax or council tax. It is the lack of either a property tax or a poll tax that would force income tax rates up.

It is worth concluding this section by noting that there is a case for also having a local tax that falls on businesses which, after all, benefit from many local services. Perhaps the most obvious choice for a local business tax is a property tax. If local authorities were allowed to collect the non-domestic property tax, then the income tax rates they would need would fall by up to 7p, but of course this would be offset by a rise in the central government's income tax rates as it would lose its present revenue from non-domestic rates. In other words, a transfer of non-domestic rates from the central government to local authorities would reduce the local need for income tax revenue and raise the central need for income tax revenue so that the overall income tax burden would be unaffected. It must be emphasised, however, that a non-domestic property tax is not a very satisfactory local tax because it has a very unequal base between local authorities. At present, there is a need for a detailed study of how best to raise local taxes from businesses.

Financing a Middle Way

Having examined the tax implications of the centralist and localist approaches, it is worth concluding by considering two other scenarios. First, suppose the Government decides to continue with the present ill-defined middle way. On this ill-defined approach, there is no clear argument for any particular level of local taxes, but perhaps a target of 4 per cent of GDP would be a reasonable one as it would cover about

111

half of local spending. Could such a yield be secured without a local income tax?

It was noted earlier that it would be possible to have a local tax yield of 4 per cent of GDP by combining a local property tax and a local poll tax, but only if the local property tax extended to non-domestic properties as well as domestic properties. However, this combination of local taxes is not very appealing. There are several reasons for this, quite apart from the special political difficulties of persisting with a poll tax at the present time. One reason is that a non-domestic property tax is not a very satisfactory local tax, as noted above. Another reason is that a domestic property tax and a poll tax, being so visible, are always likely to be especially unpopular. Why should local authorities have to raise the most unpopular taxes? If the Government is serious about wanting to be in 'partnership' with local authorities, then surely it should allow local authorities some access to an income tax which is not highly visible.

A further reason why the inclusion of both a poll tax and a domestic property tax is not very appealing is that in practice the Government is likely to want the domestic property tax to shoulder a somewhat larger share than the poll tax. Now if the dominant domestic local tax is a property tax, then it becomes very difficult to secure equity between people in different areas. This is because the domestic property tax base is very unequally distributed across the country. With the old rates, the grants scheme attempted to create equal tax rates (or 'poundages') in any two areas with comparable service levels. The result was that people in comparable homes who enjoyed comparable services paid far more in rates if they lived in high property value areas than if they lived in low property value areas. This situation was clearly not very satisfactory and it was rightly criticised by Mrs Thatcher's Government. The present Government's council tax and its associated grants will be slightly better than rates because the banding will make differences in tax payments less dramatic than differences in property values. But this banding scheme introduces its own inequities. For instance, people in a home worth 110 per cent of the average value will pay no more than people in a home worth 85 per cent of the average value. The only way of truly ameliorating the inequities of a domestic property tax are to keep its yield very low.

So, once again, the correct course seems to be a local income tax, with perhaps a modest domestic property tax as a supplement. And maybe there should be a modest local business tax as well.

Reducing the Scope of Local Government

Another possibility that seems frequently to be mooted is to remove some local functions to the central government. Before any such steps were taken, however, it would seem appropriate to examine the reasons for taking them. Such a removal might be expected to reduce variety in the public sector, and it would seem very unfortunate to undertake such a policy simply to reduce the revenue requirements of local authorities, particularly when these needs can be financed with the help of a local income tax. The one 'removal' which has some attraction is school education, but even here it depends what the central government would do. If it decided to finance all schools directly, then it is highly likely that in time it would start controlling schools—after all, it has already imposed a national curriculum on local authority schools. Consequently, the central government could end up using its new position as a near-monopolist in the supply of schooling to create very uniform schools. Moreover, it is not clear what safeguards there would be to prevent this government, or any future government, from abusing its monopoly power.

A less worrying arrangement would be one in which the central government effectively made all schools depend on fee income and helped parents to pay these fees by giving them money in the form of vouchers. The government would probably be less inclined to control schools on this arrangement since schools would be financed by parents who would be choosing what they deemed to be the best schools for their children.

If education were removed from local authorities, then local spending might fall to some 5 per cent of GDP. So a useful target yield for local taxes would be around 4 per cent. In other words, the target yield situation would be very similar to the one discussed in the last section for the middle way. As noted there, a 4 per cent yield could be secured by a property tax—on both domestic and non-domestic properties—combined with a modest poll tax; but it would be more appealing to allow local authorities to rely chiefly on a local income tax with a modest domestic property tax as a supplement, and perhaps allow them also to levy a modest tax on businesses.

Conclusion: the Need for a Local Income Tax

This paper argues that, unless the Government really seeks the centralist solution, every scenario points to the case for introducing a local income tax. It has also argued that a local income tax should not be used on its own. Columns (1) to (4) of Table 1 show that subcentral income taxes are the most important subcentral tax in OECD countries, and they show that no OECD country operates such a tax on its own (though Sweden comes very close to doing so). In other words, it seems that the general consensus in the OECD is to follow the prescriptions given here. It seems unlikely that the United Kingdom will join this consensus in the near future, but if does not, then it will probably not be long before we have yet another Green (or some other colour) Paper on local government finance.

REFERENCES

Department of the Environment (1991): *Local Government Review: A New Tax for Local Government* (Consultation Paper), DoE.

HMSO (1971): *The Future Shape of Local Government Finance* (Green Paper), Cmnd. 4741.

HMSO (1976): *Local Government Finance: Report of the Committee of Enquiry* (Layfield Committee Report), Cmnd. 6453.

HMSO (1977): *Local Government Finance* (Green Paper), Cmnd. 6813.

HMSO (1981): *Alternatives to Domestic Rates* (Green Paper), Cmnd. 8449.

HMSO (1986): *Paying for Local Government* (Green Paper), Cmnd. 9714.

8

ELECTORAL REFORM: WHAT ARE THE CONSEQUENCES?

Richard Rose

Director, Centre for the Study of Public Policy,
University of Strathclyde

Introduction

DEMOCRACY—in Abraham Lincoln's sense of 'government of the people, by the people, for the people'—is a primary value in Western political life. But it is also a value that is usually stated in terms so general that it is consistent with more than one type of electoral system. Moreover, an electoral system, whatever its attributes, cannot be judged in isolation. We not only need to consider how it works, but also what consequences the system is likely to have for the practice of government. Whereas an electoral system on its own may be judged by a standard of 'fairness', a government is likely to be judged by its 'effectiveness'.

Given two criteria for judging an electoral system—its intrinsic characteristics and its consequences—a conflict can arise, if a system deemed fairer in giving representation is reckoned to produce less effective government, and *vice versa*. Moreover, since electoral reform affects the strength of political parties in Parliament, it is inevitably a subject of partisan debate.

The constitution is the starting point for analysing electoral reform, because it decides what government is; in turn, this determines which offices are subject to popular election. All this is true of an unwritten as well as of a written constitution. The essence of democratic government is the existence of a representative assembly elected by popular vote in a free and competitive election. No more is necessary and, in Britain, without a directly elected President or regional assemblies, no more is offered.

Parliamentary Democracy's 'Unique Authority'

Parliamentary democracy gives unique authority to a popularly elected assembly, because it not only represents constituents but also determines control of the executive branch of government. By contrast, in the United States both the chief executive, the President, and Members of Congress are popularly elected. Even though the Prime Minister is not elected, Europeans regard parliamentary democracy as just as democratic as the American system. The absence of a popularly elected Second Chamber gives the House of Commons unique authority to represent the people, thus avoiding conflicts between a popularly elected Senate and House of Representatives, which can sometimes bedevil the United States Congress.

In a unitary system of government, the national government is uniquely important, with the authority to take decisions effective nationwide. By contrast, federal systems offer citizens more levels of representation. The regions in a federal system such as Germany or Canada have a popularly elected Parliament with substantial powers that can be exercised at a distance from the national capital. However, federal systems also create conflicting claims to authority: Does a regional assembly or a national assembly have a better claim to represent the people? Such a conflict cannot arise in a unitary state. The Westminster Parliament retains overriding authority to determine laws throughout the United Kingdom, including the right to change boundaries, powers and finances of local authorities or to authorise or suspend devolved regional Parliaments. Notwithstanding major differences between federal and unitary states, democracy can flourish under either type of constitution.

The right to vote in free and fair elections is necessary for democracy—but this leaves open the way in which votes are counted and converted into seats in the national Parliament. Britain uses the *first-past-the-post* system;[1] the candidate with the largest number of

---

[1] See Note 1, 'Types of Electoral Systems', below, p. 135, which defines the voting systems reviewed in this paper.

votes in a constituency becomes its MP, whether or not the person has more or less than half the vote. Other candidates get nothing. By contrast, in the multi-member constituencies of a *proportional representation* system, seats are allocated between the parties more or less in proportion to the share of the vote that each wins. For example, in a six-member constituency, a party with one-sixth of the vote gains one MP, and a party with one-third of the vote, two MPs.

First-Past-the-Post: Single-Party Government

Even if it is granted that both types of electoral system are democratic, they certainly differ in their impact on government. The first-past-the-post system normally leads to single-party government, for one party is able to win an absolute majority of MPs with less than half the popular vote. Even though no British party has won half the vote in any election since 1935, one party has won an absolute majority of seats in the House of Commons in 12 of the 13 elections since the Second World War. The consequence of a proportional representation system is the opposite: a coalition government of two or more parties is normally formed, because the division of seats in Parliament in accord with the division of votes among a multiplicity of parties means that no party has a majority.

The use of the first-past-the-post electoral system in Britain today is not a matter of choice but of inheritance. The system was established centuries before the introduction of universal suffrage. More important is the fact that the expansion of the suffrage was not matched by the introduction of proportional representation, as occurred in most European countries. Attempts were made to introduce PR before and after the First World War, but they failed. For most of the post-war era, the question of electoral reform was 'not on' politically, for successive Conservative and Labour governments were satisfied with a system that gave each in turn 100 per cent control of government with less than 50 per cent of the vote. However, since 1974, electoral reform has been on the political agenda, because the rise in the vote for a third party has threatened to return a Parliament with no one party having a majority of seats.

If Britain adopted proportional representation, government as well as elections would not be the same. Proponents of PR regard this as an additional argument in its favour. Not only would the matching of seats to votes be fairer, but also the coalition government is described as 'better government'. Most proponents of PR not only endorse a

117

change in the electoral system but also breaking the mould of two-party domination of Parliament, and in addition favour the introduction of federalism and a written Bill of Rights to constrain the power of the executive. The alleged defects of change on such a scale are part of the defence of the first-past-the-post system as an integral part of British parliamentary government as we know it.

Because electoral systems are only one part of a system of government, it is appropriate to evaluate them in terms of the impact the first-past-the-post system has on how Britain[2] is governed, and the consequences of a change to proportional representation. A person who believes it desirable to place power of government in the hands of a single party that can be held accountable by the electorate should favour the first-past-the-post system. A person who believes that coalition government is the best form of government for Britain should favour proportional representation. Although these are not the only issues involved, they remain fundamental, for any change in the electoral system will have major consequences for the political system as a whole.[3]

1. For Responsible Government, Vote First-Past-The-Post

The chief argument for the first-past-the-post system is about government, not representation. The Austrian economist, Joseph Schumpeter, defined democracy as competition between party élites for votes; he justified this with the functionalist argument: 'the rôle of the people is to produce a government'.[4] The representation of the preferences in exact proportion to popular votes is seen as less important than offering voters a clear-cut choice between a party responsible for government and an Opposition that is the alternative government. The electorate knows which party has been governing the country and can vote accordingly for the government of the day, or can turn the In party out and put the Opposition in. The system is commended because it usually manufactures a parliamentary majority

---

[2] This chapter explicitly excludes consideration of Northern Ireland, where the Westminster Parliament has imposed a system of proportional representation that it opposed for Britain.

[3] The discussion thus excludes electoral changes that would not have an impact on the political system overall, such as making election day a public holiday, modifications to the postal vote, and so on.

[4] Joseph A. Schumpeter, *Capitalism, Socialism and Democracy*, London: George Allen & Unwin, 4th edn., 1952, p. 269.

for the party with the largest share of the popular vote, whether it is at the 50 per cent mark, or as low as 40 per cent.

Defining an election as a collective choice between two and only two groups is consistent with much of the British political tradition. The idea of a strong executive opposed by a strong opposition goes back to the days of King and Court versus the Country party in the House of Commons. In the 19th century Liberals and Tories did not claim to be representative of the whole adult population; they competed as alternative teams of governing élites. Since 1918 the Conservatives and Labour have been identified with competing economic interests; the politics of In and Out is thus reckoned to parallel the politics of Us *vs.* Them.

Just as there can be more than two contenders in a first-past-the-post horse race, so there can be more than two candidates in a constituency. Yet just as there is only one winner in a horse race, so only one candidate can become a Member of Parliament under the first-past-the-post system. In 1987 a total of 283 seats were won with less than half the vote, and in 1983 and both 1974 elections more than half the seats were won by a candidate who received less than half the constituency's vote. Awarding a seat to the candidate with the largest share of the vote, even if that share is less than half, is consistent with the winner-take-all nature of power in British government, which is virtually unchecked by a second chamber or judicial review.

The first-past-the-post system is about *disproportional* representation—and proud of it. If the purpose of an election is to give voters a choice of government, then it matters little whether the party that wins all the power does so with more or less than half the popular vote. The important point is that one party wins more than half the seats in Parliament. This fixes responsibility for everything that happens during the life of the Parliament. At the end of this period, voters who are satisfied can vote to keep the governing party in office, and those who are dissatisfied can vote to turn the rascals out. This simple model of electoral competition is also consistent with contemporary theories of voting behaviour. The majority of voters do not have, nor do they wish to obtain, detailed knowledge about problems of government; that is the job of parties and their leaders. All an elector need do is form a generalised judgement of approval or disapproval of the party in power, and vote for or against more of the same.

Consensus Not Inevitable

Once in possession of a majority in the House of Commons, for the moment at least, the government of the day can do what it likes. The Opposition complaint that the government lacks a popular mandate for unpopular measures is no more relevant than the governing party's proclamation that winning 40 to 45 per cent of the vote constitutes popular endorsement of everything it does. The critical point is that a party with a manufactured parliamentary majority has the power to act—'the government's job is to govern'. For much of the post-war era it did so on a consensual middle-of-the-road platform. The rise of the Labour left and the advent of a Thatcher administration governing by conviction illustrates that consensus is not a necessary consequence of the first-past-the-post system.

Notwithstanding its rules, the first-past-the-post system manages to achieve a substantial degree of proportionality (Figure 1). One reason is that the party with the largest share of the vote nationally is bound to gain a large number of seats. The winning party boosts its share of seats about 15 per cent above its share of the popular vote. Because constituencies vary greatly in their characteristics, the official Opposition can finish first in hundreds of seats in the process of piling up a substantial share of the popular vote. In the 1980s Labour was particularly efficient; in seats it lost, it more often came third than second. Thus, Labour ended up with a bigger share of seats in the Commons than it had votes. Nationalist parties have another method for winning seats: they concentrate their vote in selected constituencies in Scotland and Wales. Plaid Cymru can come fourth in Wales as a whole, because of poor showings in South Wales, yet return MPs for Welsh-speaking seats in the North and West, and end up with an almost exact match between its share of votes and Welsh MPs (see Figure 1).

Under whatever name they fight, it is the Liberals that have consistently suffered, because their popular support is spread very evenly throughout Britain. They can win 20 or 30 per cent of the vote in hundreds of constituencies, thus gaining a substantial share of the national vote. But because Liberals have difficulty in breaking the 33·3 per cent barrier, they win few seats. If the Alliance parties had won seats in proportion to their popular vote in 1987, then they would have gained an additional 124 MPs. The Liberals and their allies are the second-place party in hundreds of constituencies. However, lacking a strong appeal to any one social group, there is no category of

Figure 1: Relation of Seats and Votes, 1987

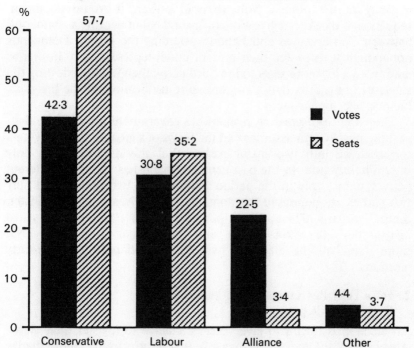

constituency where their supporters predominate to place the party first.

Because the first-past-the-post system sustains majority rule, it is sometimes argued that each MP should also be elected by a majority of votes in a constituency. This is technically possible, even when three or more candidates compete. In Australia the Alternative Vote System enables electors to rank candidates in their order of preference. If no candidate secures more than half the vote, then candidates with the least votes are eliminated and their second preferences redistributed until one candidate has an absolute majority. The French have a two-ballot system: if no candidate wins an absolute majority in the first round of an Assembly election, a second ballot is held, restricted to candidates with a substantial share of the vote. In the election of a French President, only the two top-ranking candidates in the first round proceed to the second, thus guaranteeing an absolute majority.

Requiring each MP to have an absolute majority of a constituency's

121

vote would be illogical, since the government itself does not require a majority of the popular vote to hold power. It would be inconsequential if the Alternative Vote or second ballot became a 'shoot out' between Conservatives and Labour, awarding the Liberal Democrats not enough seats to end their present under-representation. Insofar as it awarded a lot more seats to the third party, then it would destroy the single-party majority that is the strongest justification for the first-past-the-post electoral system.

The defence of creating responsible government through the first-past-the-post system assumes that the views of a great number of voters can coalesce into two major parties. Yet this assumption is only intermittently true. In the past century Britain has seen four different party systems; only in the period 1945-70 have two parties, and only two parties, monopolised the popular vote and seats at Westminster. Since February 1974 up to 30 per cent of the electorate has voted *against* both the Conservative and the Labour parties. By 1992, more than half the electorate will have voted only in multi-party elections.

2. For a Fully Representative Parliament, Vote Proportional Representation

An election is meant to give voters a chance to register their views. Advocates of PR go further; they give first priority to the representative function of democracy. This is a continuation of the Victorian struggle for the right to vote. It was not a claim that giving manual workers the vote would make for stronger or better government; it was advocated on the basis that every adult citizen (first, all males, and then women, too) had a *right* to equal representation in Parliament.[5]

The right to vote is not enough; how votes are counted and converted into seats in Parliament is considered equally important. Just as a franchise that excludes 10 per cent of the electorate from voting would be thought undemocratic, so an electoral system that denies representation to more than 10 per cent of the electorate is considered undemocratic.

The penalty that the British system imposes on parties that fail to concentrate their votes is extreme, even by the standards of other first-

---

[5] For an historical overview, see Vernon Bogdanor, *The People and the Party System: the Referendum and Electoral Reform in British Politics*, Cambridge: Cambridge University Press, 1981.

past-the-post systems. This can be measured by an Index of Disproportionality, calculated by taking the difference between 100 per cent proportionality and the degree of proportionality actually achieved. The outcome of the 1987 election was 21 per cent disproportional; the price paid for manufacturing a majority for the governing party was the denial of 136 seats in Parliament that other parties would have claimed in a system of pure proportionality.

Britain has the *most disproportional* first-past-the-post system among advanced industrial nations (Table 1). It is even more disproportional than France, which has long specialised in switching between electoral systems to favour the aims of the government of the day, and uses a first-past-the-post system to marginalise Communists and the extreme right. The operation of the British system is more than half again as disproportional as in Canada, Australia and New Zealand, and five times more disproportional than in the election of the United States House of Representatives. Whilst no system of proportional representation need be 100 per cent representative, even the least exact in converting votes into seats is substantially more proportional than the British system.

Proportional Representation and the House of Commons

Given the goal of securing a House of Commons with a close match between popular votes and popular representation in Parliament, the adoption of any system of proportional representation would be certain to produce an arithmetically more representative Parliament. The exact degree of proportionality obtained would depend upon the system adopted and upon how the parties and voters made use of it.

The first requirement of a PR system is the replacement of single-member with multi-member constituencies. Only if several representatives are returned from a single constituency can second and third place parties share in the distribution of representation. For example, if three parties divide the vote 50 per cent, 30 per cent, and 20 per cent, in the British system only the first party would be a winner. The only way in which proportionality could be achieved would be if the first party came second or third in five out of every 10 seats, the second party came first in three out of 10, and the third party came first in two out of 10. This is most unlikely to happen. In a 10-member PR constituency, the first party would take 5 seats, the second 3, and the third 2. The Index of Disproportionality would be nil.

TABLE 1
DISPROPORTIONALITY IN ELECTION OUTCOMES

	Index of Disproportionality %	Type of Electoral System
Britain	21	First past post
France	19	Single-member; double ballot
Canada	14	First past post
Australia	13	Single-member Alternative Vote
Spain	13	Proportional representation
New Zealand	12	First past post
Japan	11	First past post
Finland	11	Proportional representation
Luxembourg	9	Proportional representation
Norway	9	Proportional representation
Portugal	9	Proportional representation
Switzerland	9	Proportional representation
Belgium	8	Proportional representation
Greece	7	Proportional representation
Israel	6	Proportional representation
Denmark	5	Proportional representation
Ireland	5	STV Proportional representation
Italy	5	Proportional representation
US House of Representatives	4	First past post
Iceland	4	Proportional representation
Netherlands	4	Proportional representation
Sweden	3	Proportional representation
Germany	1	Proportional representation
Austria	1	Proportional representation
Malta	0	Proportional representation

Source: T. T. Mackie and R. Rose, *International Almanac of Electoral History*, London: Macmillan, 3rd edn., 1991, p. 510.

The fewer the number of MPs in a constituency, the greater the difficulty in maintaining exact proportionality. If a constituency had five seats, in the above example the first party's arithmetic share would be 2·5 seats and the second party's 1·5; only the third party, with 1 seat, would match seats and votes. In a four-member constituency, a new problem would arise: the first party could fairly claim 2 seats, but the second and third parties would each secure the same,

1 seat, even though they differed in their share of the vote by 10 per cent.[6]

The simplest way to avoid the problem of 'too large' remainders is to turn the whole nation into a single constituency; in this way, any party that wins 1 per cent of the vote is guaranteed at least one seat in a 100-member Parliament. The Netherlands and Israel do just this. Most countries adopt a different strategy. They have very large constituencies with up to three dozen seats and/or regional or national lists in which parties that have been disadvantaged at the constituency level can claim additional seats to bring their representation in Parliament up to their national share of the vote.

The necessity of multi-member districts in proportional representation is often advanced as a sufficient reason for rejecting PR, because it is said to undermine the link between an MP and his constituents. Such an argument ignores the fact that in hundreds of constituencies the link is negative: more than half the constituents have voted *against* their MP. Nor do British electors vote for an MP as an individual; nearly all the candidate's votes are won as the standard-bearer of a party. Nor is the vote of an MP in the House of Commons determined by constituency interests; it reflects the party whip. Even the causes that lead MPs to rebel against the whip are usually national issues, not local constituency matters.

Population growth, combined with universal suffrage, has broken the personal link between MPs and constituents that existed before 1832, when less than a hundred people often constituted the majority of votes in a borough. In a constituency of nearly 100,000 people, it is impossible for an MP to shake hands, let alone talk to, the majority of voters. It is hypocritical to suggest that MPs are chosen by their constituents. Every aspiring parliamentary candidate knows that they are chosen by local party selection committees.

Who Gets What?

A second requirement in a multi-member constituency is determining which particular candidates of a party are awarded seats. In most proportional representation systems, this is done by a party organisation; it is responsible for ranking its candidates in the order in

---

[6] For a succinct exposition of different methods of awarding seats in multi-member constituencies, including a discussion of the problem of fractional shares or 'remainders', see, for example, Thomas T. Mackie and Richard Rose, *The International Almanac of Electoral History*, London: Macmillan, 1991, pp. 503-08.

which they are to be awarded seats. If a party expects to win two or three seats in a multi-member constituency, then anyone listed first or second is virtually certain of election, and anyone listed fourth, fifth or sixth is almost certain of defeat. Voters may be given the option of altering the party's priority among candidates, but usually this does not affect the result.

The determination of the ranking of candidates on the party list must be done at the party's national headquarters when some MPs are elected on a national list. When multi-member constituencies are also defined at the regional or county level, the ranking of candidates can be done by a large constituency party, a regional party organisation or the national party headquarters, or by a combination of the three. Even when the constituency party determines the ranking, this can be an organisation covering a geographical area and population similar in size to an English county.

A degree of centralisation in the selection of MPs can enable a party to shape its parliamentary representation to reflect national party policy. A party can ensure that a given proportion of women or other minority groups is elected by giving them top places on their regional lists. It can also ensure that people it would like in Parliament for other reasons, such as suitability for a ministerial rôle, are given a high rank. Celebrities may be asked to run at the bottom of the list, in hopes that their name and fame will pull support to the party.[7]

Alternative Member System

Strengthening central party influence goes against the inclinations of most British campaigners for electoral reform; strengthening individual rather than party representation is their goal. Some proponents of reform favour the Alternative Member System (AMS), a compromise seeking to maintain hundreds of single-member districts whilst achieving the goal of proportional representation. The Federal Republic of Germany uses the Additional Member System. Electors are given two ballots, one for a representative from a single-member constituency, and the other for a party list; voters almost invariably cast both ballots for the same party. Given disproportionality in single-member constituency results, seats are distributed by PR to parties disadvantaged locally. The result is extremely proportional, but

---

[7] See my other chapter (Chapter 4) in this volume, 'The Political Economy of Cabinet Change', above, pp. 45-72.

there is little link between voters and individual representatives. The average German MP represents a constituency more than double the size of a British district, and since re-unification it is above 300,000 inhabitants.

Single Transferable Vote and PR

The best way to strengthen ties between individual electors and candidates is to combine the Single Transferable Vote (STV) with proportional representation, as is done in the Republic of Ireland. There is no party list in an Irish multi-member constituency. Instead, an elector numbers the candidates in the order of his or her preference. Since few candidates win a large mass of first preference votes, the second and subsequent preferences of voters are then redistributed until all seats have been allocated.

Most Irish voters list preferences by discriminating between candidates of the same party. The net effect is that of an American primary election within a general election. Candidates not only compete against other parties but also against their own partisan colleagues. In a five-member constituency in which a party can expect to win only one or two seats, none of the party's candidates will want to be left out. Like the American primary, Irish STV encourages members of the Irish Parliament to be more constituency-oriented than in Britain.

Whatever system of proportional representation is used, the result is almost invariably the same: no party wins a majority of seats in Parliament. The extent to which the duopoly of a two-party system is abandoned varies from country to country. In Germany, the two largest parties won 77 per cent of the vote in the last election; in Ireland, 73 per cent, and in Italy, 61 per cent. In Denmark and Belgium, the two largest parties together usually take less than half the vote, and up to a dozen different parties can win seats in Parliament. While the Westminster Parliament also has MPs representing 10 different parties, they do not hold the balance of power, because one party has an absolute majority there.

To limit the proliferation of parties, the electoral system of the Federal Republic of Germany denies representation to parties that fail to win a single-member seat or poll less than 5 per cent of the vote nation-wide. This clause makes it possible for a local or regional party to win representation, but excludes extremist parties with widespread but low levels of popular support. The clause limits the total number of parties in the German Parliament; prior to the accession of East Germany, only four parties held seats. Among this group, each is represented almost exactly in proportion to its share of the national vote.

PR = Coalition Government

The consequence of PR is predictable: coalition government. The number of parties in the coalition varies between systems. In Germany the norm is a 'little coalition' between one of the two largest parties and the Free Democrats as a junior partner. In Austria, there is often a 'big coalition' between the two largest parties. In the Benelux countries and in Italy, three or more parties may become partners in a coalition, and in Sweden four parties is the minimum required to ensure a majority to the anti-Socialist bloc. It is also possible to have a fluid coalition if a single party governs with a minority of seats. In Denmark a party with a limited number of seats can stay in office with a 'jumping majority'; important votes in Parliament are won with different allies, depending on the issue.

Proportional representation does not allow voters to choose which party wins control of government. An individual casts a ballot without knowing which parties will join as partners in a new government election. No party gets an absolute majority of seats. In about a third of elections called by a coalition government, some parties gain votes, and other coalition partners see their vote decline. Control is decided only after a more or less lengthy process of negotiation between potential partners in a coalition.[8] The process of bargaining can be called horse-trading in Ireland, and dealing in cattle in Germany. Bargaining about jobs and influence in a coalition government is not a search for the national interest, but a contest for power and for status, and it is a process from which the voters are excluded.

The need for inter-party bargaining can be evaluated as desirable, restraining the so-called 'elective dictatorship' of single-party government. The strongest party in Parliament is not strong enough to impose its programmes without the concurrence of one or more coalition partners. In the 1970s, S. E. Finer argued that 'adversary government' was inferior to coalition government because it produced too great a swing from left to right, and back again.[9] The launch of the

---

[8] See Vernon Bogdanor (ed.), *Coalition Government in Western Europe*, London: Heinemann, 1983.

[9] *Cf.* S. E. Finer (ed.), *Adversary Politics and Electoral Reform*, London: Clive Wigram, 1975, with the evidence in Richard Rose, *Do Parties Make a Difference?*, London: Macmillan, 2nd edn., 1984.

Social Democratic Party and the creation of the Alliance in 1981 were intended to 'break the mould' of British politics by introducing proportional representation and a coalition government that would have a broader base of support because it rested on more than a single party.

The introduction of any type of proportional representation system in Britain would undoubtedly produce a multi-party Parliament in which no one party could claim a majority. The only question would be: How many parties would the House divide into, and how many parties would be needed to form a government? At a minimum, at least three parties would win more than 50 seats, and possibly four. If PR had been in operation in the 1980s, then both the SDP and the Liberals would have won more than 50 seats—and no party would have come close to an absolute majority. The 1989 European Parliament election showed the potential of the Greens to win representation in the Commons.

3. Different Horses for Different Electoral Courses?

The primacy of government in justification of the first-past-the-post system prompts the question: What sort of electoral system is appropriate when the government of Britain is *not* at stake?[10] This is most obviously the case in electing the European Parliament, for control of such government as the Community has rests with the Council of Ministers of member-states and the Commission in Brussels. Whether British local government or devolved institutions for Scotland and Wales should be conceived of as representative but not governments is a debatable point.

In signing the Treaty of Rome, the British government became committed to Article 138(3), which requires that the European Parliament be elected by a 'uniform procedure'. Since 10 of the 12 member-states have proportional representation and France has adopted PR to elect its MEPS, a 'uniform procedure' can only be proportional representation. The practice of the European Community is sufficiently flexible to allow member-states to use different methods of proportional representation.

The only way in which other national governments could accept Britain's first-past-the-post system as consistent with the doctrine of

---

[10] This point is raised with great clarity in *Democracy, Representation and Elections* (1991), the Interim Report of the Labour Party's Working Party on the Electoral System, chaired by Professor Raymond Plant: see in particular pp. 91*ff.*

uniform procedure is by closing their eyes. While this was done in the first three elections, there is no assurance that it will continue. Pressures toward harmonisation within the Community are growing, and so too are pressures to make the European Parliament more important. The Westminster Parliament's authorisation of proportional representation in electing Northern Ireland's three MEPs weakens its defence. The European Court of Justice might not countenance the use of Britain's present electoral system if a legal case reached it.

A Privy Councillor could justify the co-existence of different types of electoral systems for the European Parliament and the Westminster Parliament, since the Strasbourg body is not asked to form a government. The contrast might even be interpreted as evidence of the superiority of Westminster, because it has produced a single-party government that the electorate could hold accountable.

Devolution: A Scots Parliament?

Devolution poses the issue of electoral reform for a putative Scots Parliament. One logical argument for proportional representation in Edinburgh is that devolution is about increasing the importance of representation, and reducing the centralisation of authority in the hands of a single party. The first-past-the-post system has consistently produced a much more disproportional result than in England. In 1987, for example, Labour won 69 per cent of Scotland's seats at Westminster with only 42 per cent of the vote, a greater degree of disproportionality than that of the Conservatives in England. Overall, Scots MPs had an Index of Disproportionality of 27 per cent.

However, if devolution is about creating a government held accountable by Scottish voters, then the first-past-the-post system would appear more appropriate, for it would manufacture a majority for a single party in an Edinburgh Parliament. It would be consistent with its interest as well as logic for a Westminster Parliament with a Labour majority to approve the first-past-the-post system for devolved Parliaments, since Labour, while it has never won half the vote at a Westminster election in Scotland, normally runs well ahead of its rivals and would expect to win manufactured majorities.

In a hung Parliament, a minority Labour government would find itself facing immediate difficulties about an electoral system for a Scots Parliament. Liberal Democrats would press very hard to elect the Parliament by proportional representation. Conservatives could accept this as a guarantee of more seats than the party would be likely to win in its present parlous state there. Furthermore, Conservatives could argue for proportional representation of nations at Westminster, that is, reducing the number of Scots MPs by about 15 so that Scotland's share of parliamentary representation became the same as its share of the United Kingdom population.

Strengthening the defence of Union is another argument in favour of proportional representation for a Scots Parliament. In a Scots Parliament, Labour cannot be guaranteed a permanent majority. If the Scottish National Party (SNP) became the official Opposition, then in a first-past-the-post system the swing of the electoral pendulum could manufacture a majority for the Nationalists. The SNP could claim that, having played the game by the rules laid down in London, it deserved the right to use its control of government in Scotland to advance to independence.

A Welsh Assembly?

A Parliament or Assembly for Wales presents a different type of electoral issue. For the foreseeable future, the outcome would not be in doubt, for Labour has won more than half the Welsh *seats* in Parliament at every general election since 1935, although it has not won more than half the popular *vote* in Wales since 1970. Concern in Wales would not be about Welsh Nationalists winning power due to the swing of the electoral pendulum; it would be about permanent one-party government in Cardiff.

In its day, the Northern Ireland Parliament at Stormont had powers analogous to those proposed for devolved assemblies in Scotland and Wales. It also had a permanent one-party majority, for as long as the electorate voted on grounds of national and religious identity, then an electorate that was two-thirds British and Protestant was certain to elect a Unionist government. When the troubles arose in 1969, an investigation by the independent Cameron Commission, appointed by the British government, concluded that one cause of the troubles there was the existence of a permanent one-party government.[11]

The issue of one-party control also arises in local government in England.[12] In a unitary state, local government may be considered

---

[11] Cameron Commission, *Disturbances in Northern Ireland*, Belfast: HMSO, Cmnd. 532, 1969.

[12] For a provocative argument about its evils, see Mike Squires and Mark Cowling, 'Normal British Misconduct', *Politics*, Vol. 11, No. 1 (April 1991), pp. 3-7.

weak; therefore, one-party control can be dismissed as unimportant as long as the actions of local authorities are deemed unimportant. When they raised issues of national significance, as in the 1980s, the Westminster government showed it was ready to use its national majority to alter local government boundaries and finance. Thus, alternation in power at Westminster can provide a substitute for alternation of power in town halls, by imposing national policy on local authorities that are dominated by a single party.

The more power is decentralised to reformed local authorities or to Scottish or Welsh Parliaments, the greater the significance of the choice of an electoral system, for the new authorities would not be agents of a Westminster government, but powers in their own right. This means that the alternation of power at Westminster would be insufficient to guarantee an important benefit of Schumpeterian electoral competition, namely, the capacity of voters to turn a local government out. In a one-party area, the alternative is not another party in power, but coalition. To argue that a coalition is sufficient to offer voters a choice in Scotland or Wales, or in Durham or Wiltshire, inevitably raises questions about Westminster, too.

4. Principles and Practice

The predictability of the consequences of proportional representation sharpens the conflict about electoral reform. Just as there is no way in which present defenders of the first-past-the-post electoral system can dodge the fact that responsible government is gained at the price of disproportional representation, so there is no way for proponents of PR to hide the fact that its introduction would not only reduce the present disproportion between seats and votes but also weaken the link between voters and the choice of government.

If one believes in the virtues of centralising authority in a unitary government in which legislative and executive powers are fused in a Cabinet accountable to Parliament, then the first-past-the-post system can be supported as contributing to this result. Equally, if one agrees with the authors of the American Constitution that more checks make for a better balanced government, then adopting proportional representation would, within a parliamentary framework, place the check of coalition upon single party government.

A more complicated set of questions arises if one concludes that an electoral system should compensate or counterbalance other attributes of the constitution. In Eastern Europe citizens have been subject to an overbearing authoritarian government for more than two generations. It is appropriate to adopt proportional representation there, since this is the best guarantee against the dominance of any party, democratic or undemocratic. In Britain, anyone who fears over-concentration of power should favour proportional representation in order to create coalition government. Coalition is a more immediately attainable goal than a justiciable Bill of Rights or a written Constitution. Moreover, its effects are more pervasive.

However, if proposals to decentralise authority from Westminster take effect, then a single-party government produced by the first-past-the-post electoral system could be defended as preventing the complete fragmentation of authority. For example, a devolved authority in Edinburgh that was a squabbling coalition would speak with less authority in London, or outside Britain. The development of effective vertical relations between more independent local and regional authorities and Westminster would require continuous bargaining between the centre and the new decentralised authorities. Coalition government makes this more difficult, because the first requirement of local leaders is to maintain their local coalition. It also makes bargaining more difficult because no side can be sure that other parties will deliver their share of the bargain.

Parties, Votes, PR and Power

Any discussion that denies a rôle to the concerns of political parties is academic in the pejorative sense. Major changes in the practice of government cannot occur against the wishes of a majority in Parliament. A hung Parliament would force all parties to think seriously about electoral reform, albeit under conditions of considerable uncertainty, for no one party could deliver the votes needed to secure change.

Even if party leaders agree, MPs may hesitate about abandoning an electoral system that has brought them to Parliament and adopting a new system that threatens to remove more than 100 of their number from Parliament. Increasing the size of the House of Commons to 750 or 800 seats might be necessary to re-assure nervous backbenchers that there could still be a place for them in a House of Commons elected by PR.

If parties split on the introduction of PR, a referendum could be called to resolve the impasse. A referendum would enable leaders of both the Conservative and Labour parties to campaign together to oppose PR. If that happened, an electorate that remains inclined to the two established parties would probably endorse the *status quo*. However, if one of the two big parties as well as the Liberal Democrats favoured PR, it would have a good chance of carrying in a referendum.

If the past two decades remain the pattern, parties at Westminster will continue to muddle through. The electorate will tolerate a great deal of muddle or inconsistency, for the *sine qua non* of a democracy is not how the votes are counted, but that a free election is held to choose the nation's government.

NOTE 1

Types of Electoral Systems

Simple plurality or first-past-the-post

The candidate with the largest number of votes in a constituency becomes its MP. If only two candidates contest a single-member constituency, then the winner necessarily has an absolute majority. If more than two candidates contest a seat, the winner may have an absolute majority (that is, more than half the vote) or simply a plurality (that is, at least one vote more than the candidate finishing second).' The first-past-the-post system is in use in the Westminster Parliament and throughout the Old Dominions, and in the election of the United States Congress.

Proportional representation

Seats are allocated to parties according to their percentage share of the vote. This requires multi-member constituencies, so that representation can be divided among two or more parties. In addition, most proportional representation systems also have very large regional or national constituencies that provide seats for parties that have failed to get their proportional share of seats in a multi-member constituency. For example, if a constituency has only six members of Parliament and seven parties win votes there, at least one must be left out in the award of seats. Most proportional representation systems set a threshold requiring a party to win a minimum share of votes to participate in the sharing-out process. Some form of proportional representation is used in the great majority of countries in Western Europe, and now also in Eastern Europe.

Single transferable vote (STV)

A voter ranks candidates in order of preference, first, second, third, etc. In *STV proportional representation*, the first preferences are counted, and if a candidate has more votes than required for the award of a seat, then the surplus votes are transferred to other candiates in accord with the second preferences of those voting for the winner. Votes for candidates whose share of the vote is too small to win a seat are also transferred according to second preferences. This system is in use in the Republic of Ireland and in Northern Ireland for electing assemblies and representation in the European Parliament. It is endorsed by the Liberal Democrats. When the winning candidate in a *first-past-the-post* system is required to have an absolute majority, each voter can be asked to mark an STV ballot. The second preferences of the lowest-ranking candidates are then redistributed until one candidate has an absolute majority. This is the rule in Australia.

Additional member system

A hybrid of the first-past-the-post and proportional systems, in which half the members of Parliament can be elected in single-member constituencies by a simple plurality, and the other half by proportional representation from regional or national constituencies. This system is in use in the Federal Republic of Germany; the overall effect is proportional. It has been proposed for use in Britain by a committee of the Hansard Society.

NOTE 2

A Note on Sources

In addition to the books cited in footnotes, an interested reader may want to note the following. For definitive statistics on British election results, F. W. S. Craig, *British Electoral Facts, 1832-1987*, Aldershot: Dartmouth, 1989. For analyses of principles and theories of electoral systems, Enid Lakeman, *How Democracies Vote: A Study of Majority and Proportional Electoral Systems*, London: Faber & Faber, 3rd edn., 1970, and Rein Taagepera and Matthew Soberg Shugart, *Seats and Votes: The Effects and Determinants of Electoral Systems*, New Haven: Yale University Press, 1989.

Discussions of particular countries are found in Andrew McLaren Carstairs, *A Short History of Electoral Systems in Western Europe*, London: George Allen & Unwin, 1980, and Vernon Bogdanor and David Butler (eds.), *Democracy and Elections: Electoral Systems and their Political Consequences*, Cambridge: Cambridge University Press, 1983. Wide-ranging discussions of aspects of electoral reform are found in Arend Lijphart and Bernard Grofman (eds.), *Choosing an Electoral System*, New York: Praeger, 1984, and Bernard Grofman and Arend Lijphart (eds.), *Electoral Laws and their Political Consequences*, New York: Agathon, 1986.

9

ECONOMIC AND POLITICAL LIBERALISM

Richard Holme

IT IS A STRIKING paradox that the re-discovery in the 1980s by the Conservative Government of the merits of economic liberalism was not matched by any parallel enthusiasm for political liberalism. Indeed, in many ways political liberalism, with its emphasis on constitutionalism, human rights, free speech and democratic participation, was seen by the Prime Minister, Mrs Thatcher, as a distraction from, or even a positive barrier to, the liberation of the market in Britain.

The domestic qualification is important. For, in the context of the emergence of Central and Eastern Europe from the shadow of totalitarianism, the then Prime Minister was one of the first to see the connection between the free market and the free individual, between the commercial and the civil society. *Glasnost* and *perestroika* were accepted as the necessary twin-tracks for progress in Gorbachev's Soviet Union as readily by the British government as by the rest of the West.

It is interesting to note that latterly this linkage has even become the received wisdom of overseas development policy in Britain. Aid to Third World countries is now officially to be linked to progress on democracy and human rights, which are not merely seen as desirable in themselves but as pre-conditions for economic progress. Freedom and growth are seen to be what a *Financial Times* leading article called 'Siamese twins'.

Whether such linkage, which does seem broadly to correspond to the most dynamic interpretation of Western experience over the past three hundred years, is intrinsic and proven may be arguable. Some would point to Chile or South Korea or even to Nazi Germany in the 1930s as instances of countries where authoritarian governments have presided over relative economic success.

Economic and Political Liberalism: The Close Connection

What is not arguable, however, is the close intellectual and philosophical connection between economic and political liberalism. This might at least infer that the two systems of thought co-exist more naturally together than other combinations.

The purpose of this essay is to trace the resemblances between a free market and a democratic polity, to show that the analogy is comprehensive and striking, and to suggest that it cannot be ignored by those who, like the Institute of Economic Affairs, are committed to economic freedom.

What are the principal characteristics of a successful market? I would summarise them in a series of propositions.

○ *First, that markets are in a fundamental sense egalitarian,* not discriminating between participants on the basis of extraneous status.

○ *Second, that the market is led by customer choice,* to which alternative suppliers respond competitively.

○ *Third, that the customer has the necessary information to make valid choices* and that ignorance does not represent a barrier.

○ *Fourth, that access to the market is fairly open* to both customers and suppliers.

○ *Finally, that the market is regulated* to the degree necessary to secure openness, fairness and the overriding rights of the customer.

These propositions can be translated, albeit approximately, into the political sphere. Before scrutinising them one by one, testing how far the citizen can count on the same dominating position in British society as the customer notionally enjoys in a 'perfect' free market, it may be worth a brief excursus to consider the nature of the British political system as a whole.

Proponents of the unwritten British constitution have often argued that flexibility and adaptability to change are conspicuous advantages of a system based on conventions and understandings rather than on legalistic rules. This comforting argument has been belied, at least in modern times, by the inertia with which various constitutional challenges have been met. For instance, Britain has switched from a two-party system in the immediate post-war period to a three- or even multi-party system today without any attempt at electoral reform to reflect the new reality. In Scotland a popular and general wish for a substantial measure of self-government has run into the immovable object of a centralised unitary state which does not know how to devolve. Freedom of information, a legitimate citizen entitlement in any bottom-up democratic society, has proved incompatible with secretive top-down government, hedged in, as Whitehall is, by executive prerogatives and official secrecy.

Perhaps most conspicuously of all, as Britain adjusts painfully to the new Europe it has become apparent that the British governmental system, used to hugging all power to itself, has no inclination to share it—nor even the constitutional vocabulary which would allow fruitful discussions of such issues as subsidiarity or shared sovereignty.

The British Constitution: Inflexibility of History and Tradition

The system is inflexible for the same reason which accounts for its relative lack of openness and democracy. The reason is that we have in Britain a constitution which derives its main legitimacy from history and tradition rather than from any contractual notion of the people banding together for their common purposes.

All the language speaks of sovereignty, originally of the Crown and now of the Crown-in-Parliament, and of subjecthood. We have no foundation of consent and contract between free citizens. Instead we have the continuity of top-down power, wrapped still in the ceremonious 'mysterie' of medieval monarchy.

This intrinsic institutional conservatism makes each step of reform difficult, a wresting-away from the centre rather than a redistribution of voluntarily shared power; not the rational re-negotiation of a consensual contract but a perceived threat to the foundations of the whole top-heavy edifice of power.

So it seems that, unlike a market which is driven by the restless search of customers for the best and is, therefore, as a consequence, innovative, our constitution is relatively inflexible and unadaptable. The British political system is also hierarchical, still based to an extraordinary degree compared to other democracies on prerogative and patronage. In this respect it again differs from a successful market which is basically egalitarian.

The use of 'egalitarian' as a description of a market needs some qualification.

Clearly free markets do not tend to equality of outcome. They tend to favour those who are quickest on their feet. Since this leads to inequality many people are concerned with the redistribution of these outcomes in the social and economic spheres. Indeed, in an age when capitalism is seen to have won definitively the argument with socialism, it is the basis of this redistribution rather than attempts to abolish or curtail the market which forms the main stuff of political debate.

However, in another sense a perfect market is egalitarian. All may buy and sell. There is no special position or hierarchy outside the transaction. Thus there is equal access and equal status in the marketplace. There can be no sovereign and no subjects, only a universal freedom to deal with each other.

By contrast, there is no presumption of equality of status built into the British system. In the political culture the notion of citizenship, ancient as the Greeks, is still novel to a nation of subjects riddled by class differentiation and social hierarchy. In the British constitution there is no Bill of Rights putting the universal rights of equal citizens first and permanent in all things. Even the relatively modest attempts to incorporate the European Convention on Human Rights into UK law, 'repatriating our rights', has met with strong opposition from an unholy alliance between some MPs frightened of a loss of parliamentary sovereignty and a Whitehall system which finds administration easier if government can remain, in certain crucial respects, above the law and difficult to challenge.

Markets Are Driven by Choice

Markets are not only about equality of status but, according to my second characterisation, they are also about choice. Indeed, markets are *driven* by choice. Yet what choice does the British electoral system offer the voter which is not loaded? First-past-the-post voting tends to resolve each contest into a two-horse race. In national elections this creates duopoly since a third party can make no breakthrough unless it achieves over one-third of the votes, at which point it will displace one of its competitors and become a duopolist itself, as happened when Labour displaced the Liberals in the 1920s.

Electoral duopoly suited hard-line ideologists of the era dominated by Communist-derived ideas of class war very well. They could represent that the individual, and society, had only one choice, 'for' or 'against' their version of Utopia. So the British electoral system and ideological conflict were made for each other.

Yet the world which is emerging from the shadow of collectivism is becoming less polarised and more pluralistic. It is no accident that the countries of Eastern and Central Europe, like the countries of the Iberian peninsula and Greece 10 years before them, have not leapt from totalitarianism to electoral duopoly, from one party to two. They have all chosen proportional representation which allows several strands of political engagement to emerge but then weaves them together in an alternating tapestry of conflict and co-operation. Continental European politics are negotiation politics, rather than the winner-takes-all imposition of 'elective dictatorship' based on minority popular support with which the British have had to make shift.

For several decades support for the two major parties has been confined to about three-quarters of the vote, despite a system favouring duopoly. It is surely time that competition was allowed to emerge fully in order to galvanize the market-place rather than being suppressed by a self-serving cartel.

The Problem of Governmental Secrecy

There is, however, a further barrier to the participation of the citizen/voter in the political market-place and it lies in the absurd secrecy which cloaks British government. Official secrecy is clearly a legacy of top-down government which may have been 'of the people' and, at its paternalistic best, is sometimes 'for the people' but has never really become 'by the people' because by its very nature it is nothing of the sort.

The fact that legislators, the citizens' representatives in the governmental system, are unable to secure relevant information on public policy choices and processes, makes any attempt at either pre-legislative deliberation or even effective scrutiny by Parliament more difficult. Even more seriously, the citizens themselves, without freedom of information and with no end to official secrecy, are vouchsafed no more than glimpses of a system which is supposed to belong to them but in which their understanding and choices are constrained and in which any sense of 'ownership' is therefore fatally lacking.

(It is interesting to note parenthetically how different this deliberate official concealment is from current practice in the best industrial companies, for instance, where open communication lines and good information flows are essential to employee grasp and commitment.)

Britain's culture of official secrecy looks increasingly inappropriate in a modern educated democracy, and in a well-run market-place would certainly be seen as attempts to obfuscate the consumer.

The combination of a duopolistic electoral system, the absence of universal rights and the maintenance of official secrecy all tend to the same end which is a lower level of informed participation in the political market-place. The popular sense of alienation from the political process reflected in several attitude surveys which show a lack of confidence both in institutions and leadership is symptomatic of a belief that, instead of the system being rational and open to all, it is rigged to deny effective access to many. Even a vote is seen warily by many as a symbolic act which probably will not make much difference rather than being the proud expression of an important right to choose, for which previous generations had to fight.

British government is seen by all too many of our fellow citizens as a closed system which belongs permanently to 'them' rather than being fully owned by 'us'. Politics has become a restricted market-place which most visit as rarely as possible and some never at all.

An Open, Fair and Consumer-Led Market-Place

My final criterion of a successful market-place is that it should be regulated in order to secure openness, fairness and the rights of the customer. In the political sphere in Britain this is a long way short of being the case.

So great is the level of partisanship in an adversarial system that many British politicians in contemporary society seem to find it difficult to distinguish between the game of politics and the rules by which it is conducted. The game tends to overflow the field and the only rule has become to get away with it, in the crude sense of the government being able to command a majority in the appropriate division in the House of Commons. In a reverse of the classic description of the American system, we have a government of men not laws.

There is a deep suspicion in Britain, itself the inspired inventor of a hundred games and their rule-books, of writing down in legalistic language the rules of the greatest game of all, the way we govern ourselves.

Yet just as an unregulated market will tend to exploitation, monopoly and abuse, so British government degenerates without proper checks and balances, rules and prescribed processes. We lack the vigilance which freedom is said to require.

Central and Local Government—A Morass

To take but one example, the relationship between central and local government in Britain, even leaving aside the position of Scotland and Wales, is a morass into which democracy, efficiency and public finance are all sinking. A constitutional analysis is needed rather than still more short-term jockeying for political advantage. That would require recognition that both levels of institution have a permanent and valuable place in our affairs, as the European Charter of Local Self Government which Britain refuses to sign would have us do, and would then proceed to a definition of respective structure and functions, of the way they interlock and the manner in which conflicts shall be resolved. Financing, which is complicated enough in all conscience, would succeed not precede this constitutional definition and be consonant with it.

Merely to describe this rational approach, which would be self-evident in any constitutionally respectful democracy, is to indicate the scale of the British problem.

It is not surprising that many reformers, such as the Institute for Public Policy Research, Charter 88 and Lord Scarman, have led their agenda for reform with a demand for a written constitution. Yet perhaps this brief essay has indicated that the British malaise is too deep-seated to be cured simply by writing down the prescription.

If I am a step-by-step incremental reformer, starting with proportional representation not merely for its own benefits but because it is the means for successive reforms, it is at least in part because I believe Britain needs a change of political culture as well as of political system. Each reform, as it was discussed, during parliamentary deliberation, and in practice once enacted, could serve to articulate constitutional values, to educate and gradually to assert popular ownership in that which the present system has deprived people of— *their own government.*

Towards the end of that process a written constitution would become not only desirable but essential, as a codification of the new settlement.

If Britain pursues economic liberalism without political liberalism in parallel, embodying that liberalism in truly democratic constitutional principles, then my fear is that our growth will be stunted and that we shall fail to liberate the full potential of our society. Constitutional questions are not now, if they have ever been, academic; they are central to our future.

THE AUTHORS

Stephen Haseler is Professor of Government at the City of London Polytechnic and holds a Visiting Professorship at the University of Maryland. He is Co-Chairman of the Radical Society, founded by, amongst others, Norman Tebbit, Brian Walden, Lords Chapple and Chalfont, and Neville Sandelson. He is a former Labour candidate and GLC Committee Chairman, a founder member of the SDP and Chairman of the Social Democratic Alliance. His books include *The Gaitskellites* (1969), *The Death of British Democracy* (1976), *Eurocommunism* (1978), and *The Tragedy of Labour* (1979). He is a regular contributor to *Encounter* and *The Independent*.

Richard Holme (Lord Holme of Cheltenham, CBE) has been actively involved in constitutional issues for nearly two decades. He is a former director of the National Committee for Electoral Reform and Chairman of the Rights Campaign, and is currently Secretary of the Parliamentary Democracy Trust and Chairman of the Constitutional Reform Centre.

For some years he was an Associate Member of Nuffield College, Oxford; and he is the author of *The People's Kingdom* (1987) and co-editor of *1688-1988: Time for a New Constitution* (1989).

Lord Holme is a Liberal Democrat member of the House of Lords and Vice-Chairman of his party's Federal Policy Committee.

Lord Hunt of Tanworth, GCB, was Secretary of the Cabinet from 1973 to 1979 and prior to that had been concerned with management questions in both the Treasury and the Civil Service Department. Since leaving the Civil Service he has been Chairman of both the Prudential Corporation (1985-90) and the Banque Nationale de Paris plc (1980-).

David King studied economics at Oxford University and at York University where his D.Phil. thesis concerned local taxation. He was later economics consultant to the Royal Commission on the

Constitution. Since 1978 he has been at Stirling University where he is now a Senior Lecturer. In 1982 he was a Visiting Fellow at the Australian National University in Canberra. In 1986-88 he was consultant on local tax reform in Portugal. In 1987-88 he was seconded as economic adviser on local tax reform to the Department of the Environment. He is currently leading an OECD project to advise 'European Economies in Transition' on fiscal federalism.

Dr King's publications include: (with Alan Maynard) *Rates or Prices?* (Hobart Paper No. 54, IEA, 1972), *Taxes on Immovable Property* (OECD, 1983), *Fiscal Tiers: The Economics of Multi-level Government* (1984); and he was editor of *Local Government Economics in Theory and Practice* (1991), and of *Fiscal Federalism in European Economies in Transition* (OECD, forthcoming).

Graham Mather has been General Director of the Institute of Economic Affairs since 1987. By training a lawyer, he was educated at Hutton Grammar School and New College, Oxford, where he was Burnet Law Scholar. Prior to joining the IEA he was head of the Institute of Directors Policy Unit.

Graham Mather writes, broadcasts and lectures widely on economic, business and public policy issues. In 1989 he was appointed a member of the Monopolies and Mergers Commission. His specific research interests include competition policy, the labour market and industrial relations, and European constitutional issues. In the field of public administration he has delivered papers and lectures to the Royal Institute of Public Administration, the Institute of Local Government Studies and the Association of First Division Civil Servants. For the IEA he has recently edited and introduced *Europe's Constitutional Future* (IEA Readings No. 33, 1990).

Gerard Radnitzky is Emeritus Professor of the Philosophy of Science in the University of Trier, Germany; formerly Professor of the Philosophy of Science at the Ruhr-University Bochum, and Associate Professor at the University of Gothenburg, Sweden. He is *Membre Titulaire* of the *Académie Internationale de Philosophie des Sciences* and a member of the Mont Pèlerin Society. Among his publications are *Contemporary Schools of Metascience* (1968, 1973), *Preconceptions in Research* (1974), *Epistemologia della ricerca* (1978), *Entre Wittgenstein et Popper* (1987), and over 160 papers in the philosophy of science and in political philosophy.

Richard Rose is director of the Centre for the Study of Public Policy, University of Strathclyde, Glasgow. In the course of more than three decades he has been a Visiting Fellow at the American Enterprise Institute and The Brookings Institution, Washington DC; a Visiting Professor at the Wissenschaftszentrum Berlin, European University Institute, Florence, and Johns Hopkins University, Baltimore, Maryland, and a consultant to the OECD. His books and papers have been translated into 12 languages, and he has lectured in more than two dozen countries on five continents. Among his three dozen books are: *Understanding Big Government: The Programme Approach* (1984); *Ordinary People in Public Policy: A Behavioural Analysis* (1989); *Electoral Behaviour: A Comparative Handbook* (1974); *Do Parties Make a Difference?* (1980); *The Problem of Party Government* (1974); *Politics in England* (1965); and *The Postmodern President: The White House Meets The World* (1988).

Frank Vibert was educated at Oundle School and the University of Oxford (First Class Honours in PPE, 1963). He was a Senior Research Fellow at the Institute of Economic Affairs, 1989-90, and is now its Deputy Director. He was a Senior Fellow with the World Institute for Development Economics Research at the United Nations University in Helsinki, Finland, 1989-91. He was formerly a Principal Administrator, Economics and Statistics Department, at the Organisation for Economic Co-operation and Development, Paris, 1965-67; Program Officer, Senior Economist, Adviser and Senior Adviser with the World Bank, Washington DC, 1967-87. His publications include contributions to *Europe's Constitutional Future* (IEA Readings No. 33, 1990).

Competition or Credit Controls?

DAVID T. LLEWELLYN and MARK HOLMES

The 1980s experienced one of the fastest growth rates of lending to the personal sector of any decade this century. Personal sector debt rose by around £350 billion and lending to the personal sector expanded at an average annual rate of 19 per cent. The decade was also a period of major deregulation, structural change, and enhanced competition in the financial system. Although inflation was reduced sharply early in the decade, it accelerated in the later years. One of the factors identified by the Bank of England as contributing to the latter acceleration was 'a massive increase in the availability of credit, whose roots can be traced back to the lifting of a series of restrictions on lending institutions in the early 1980s'.

This relaxation of controls over the financial system is central to understanding both why there was the surge in credit and whether controls would be effective in the future. Easing regulation made the financial system more competitive as different sectors of the market were no longer segregated from each other.

This increase in competition had its customary effect, lowering prices and widening the range of financial services available. Not surprisingly, demand surged especially from the tightly restricted personal sector. This surge in demand was channelled primarily through the housing market causing a disequilibrium or stock-adjustment process.

In this *Hobart Paper*, David Llewellyn and Mark Holmes argue that such a process of stock adjustment is likely to be insensitive to price but that, once it is over, the rate of growth of credit from its new level would once again be controllable by price (i.e. interest rates). Market conditions which have revived interest in credit controls among politicians, journalists and academics, were temporary and have now disappeared.

Hobart Paper 117

ISBN 0-255 36300-1

£7.95

The Institute of Economic Affairs
2 Lord North Street, Westminster
London SW1P 3LB
Telephone: 071-799 3745